THE LITTLE SABOTEUR

*Marco von Münchhausen*

# THE LITTLE SABOTEUR

*Get things done in life by conquering
your weaker self*

*Illustrated by Gisela Aulfes*

**CYAN** CAMPUS

Copyright © 2005 Campus Verlag GmbH, Frankfurt/Main

First published in German as *So zähmen Sie Ihren inneren Schweinehund!: Vom ärgsten Feind zum besten Freund* by Campus Verlag, Frankfurt/Main, 2002

This translation first published in Great Britain in 2005 by
Cyan/Campus Books, an imprint of

Cyan Communications Limited
4.3 The Ziggurat
60–66 Saffron Hill
London
EC1N 8QX
www.cyanbooks.com

A CIP record for this book is available from the British Library

ISBN 1-904879-04-7

Translated and typeset by Cambridge Publishing Management
(Translators: Susan James and Christine Shuttleworth)

Printed and bound in Great Britain by
TJ International, Padstow, Cornwall

# CONTENTS

# Introduction

There was a sense of great anxiety at the most recent conference of the little saboteurs. This is usually an occasion noted for plenty of relaxation and good fun. It is one of the high points of the saboteurs' year. The conference takes place at the beginning of August, when most people are on holiday and therefore don't notice that their little saboteur has once again abandoned them for a few days. Here the saboteurs compare notes about their experiences and inform each other about the latest trends. The most eagerly awaited event is the prizegiving for the best new tricks for complicating or even confounding people's best intentions. For this is precisely one of their favorite occupations: interfering with the plans of their masters and mistresses. These little troublemakers are mostly invisible as they go about their business, and only noticeable in the form of inner resistance or an inner voice.

So, this year, all the saboteurs present at the conference were very nervous. An ominous rumor was spreading, and everyone was waiting tensely to hear what their special reporter had to announce. Finally he stepped onto the platform, and an expectant silence filled the hall. What he had to tell them was, for most of them, even worse than they had feared.

After many years of their virtually unchallenged position in the background of everyday human life, a book about them, researched by *humans, was about to be published, a book about the so-called little saboteur. Most of those present became rigid with fear and turned pale as the special reporter continued to explain. In this work, he had discovered, their fields of action would be revealed, all their tricks and tactics exposed, and—worst of all—readers would be offered strategies for conquering and even taming their inner saboteurs.*

*Cries of outrage were heard from the assembled crowd. According to everything he had heard, the speaker continued, the portrayal of their tricks was so accurate and the recommendations for dealing with them were so practical and promising that they could only be based on insider information. The suspicion of a sophisticated espionage system, even treachery among their own ranks, immediately arose. It was agreed that efforts should be made as soon as possible to get hold of the manuscript of the book before publication, in order to decide on further measures to be taken at a special conference in three months' time.*

Of course, this book would have been published much earlier if it hadn't been for the author's own little saboteur! How on earth did the saboteur manage to ensure that the author would keep postponing his writing of the book? It's a mystery. After all, most people like being written about—but not the little saboteur. He knows perfectly well that his tricks will be exposed and that the readers will find out how to keep him under control—and that's something no saboteur wants.

The little saboteur in us usually rears his ugly head just when we are trying to change our bad habits or finally get to grips with a continually postponed project. But even when we have made the required effort to make a change or translate our ideas into action, he never rests, but tries all possible means to make us abandon our efforts yet again. His arguments are commonplace, yet at the same time brilliantly seductive, since they are direct and plausible, and usually include the promise of a temporary respite or satisfaction.

In this book, of course, we are also considering your own personal saboteur! Which is just what the little troublemaker sensed when you thought of buying this book. Perhaps he tried to dissuade you from the purchase? He may have concocted compelling arguments such as "No time for reading" or "What's the use?" At any rate, this time it was you, not he, who chalked up a victory. Or was your saboteur simply caught unawares because you received this book as a present? That would have annoyed him quite considerably. The fact that you have started reading it, by the way, is the first sign of success on your part—you have taken an important step, after which the rest won't be nearly as difficult.

By reading this book, you will acquire important information to help you deal with your own little saboteur.

In **Part I** you will learn *in which areas* of our everyday lives these little nuisances are active and where they are constantly frustrating our efforts. You will have a chance to work out the *activity profile of your own personal saboteur*, in order to find out what opportunities he may seize to cause you trouble.

In **Part II** you will obtain insight into the saboteur's multifarious *box of tricks*. In the process you will come to realize how many diverse and subtle methods our little enemies can make use of to bring our plans crashing to the floor, and which are the *favorite sayings and tactics of your own little saboteur*. This realization alone will help you not to be taken in so often by his attempts at sabotage.

In **Part III**, finally, you will be shown *the best way to deal with your own little saboteur* in order to achieve your intentions and goals with greater success and less effort. The strategies described are not designed to help you in a permanent struggle with your saboteur (a battle that in any case you can never entirely win), but to tame him, even to transform him from an enemy into a friend and ally. In the future, you will be able to deal more efficiently and economically with a previously annoying partial aspect of your personality, and perhaps even end up walking hand-in-hand through life with your little saboteur.

# Part I

# The Little Saboteur in Everyday Life

It happened yesterday evening—he got me again. Once again I wanted to go jogging after work. I had already got my sports gear and stopwatch out of the wardrobe, but my little saboteur got his teeth into me and dragged me to the sofa in such a determined fashion that I had to give up the struggle—I stayed indoors. Result: today I'm plagued by my bad conscience because of my lack of willpower.

Sound familiar, does it—the battle with your little saboteur? It's that indescribable inner resistance that we need to overcome every time we want to make a change in our lives.

Just what is this force that keeps stopping us from trying something new? Why have so many of our New Year resolutions melted away like the winter snow by mid-January? Of course—it's that little saboteur. *He is gobbling up our good resolutions. That's why New Year's Day is the Festival of the Little Saboteur!* All the good resolutions we make for the New Year make his mouth water—hardly ever does he get so much fodder.

In my public lectures I often recall the following experiment:

The leader of the research group placed a glass panel in a tank full of piranhas, at a time when all the piranhas had moved to one side of the tank to feed. Then the fish began to swim back towards the other side, but came up against the glass panel, which they couldn't detect because it was transparent. Time and again they took a run at it, but each time they experienced pain from the impact with the glass. In time they learned to change their ways and swam only as far as a short distance from the glass panel, in order to make full use of at least the space that still remained to them—and they got used to it. After a few weeks the glass panel was removed. You would have expected the piranhas to be delighted and to start swimming again in the part of the tank that had previously

been off limits for them. But no—I expect you have guessed what happened—just as before, the fish swam only to the center of the tank and then turned around. They had learned their lesson: "This is it—this is as far as we can go."

We keep meeting exactly the same phenomenon in our everyday lives—the "invisible limits" in us that stop us from using all the opportunities presented to us, developing our full potential and allowing our good intentions to be realized. The guard on duty at these invisible frontiers is often our little saboteur, and whenever we set out to cross them (in order to move from the familiar "comfort zone" into the zone of personal growth), we hear a familiar voice in our ear: "Look, don't bother, it's too much of an effort." "Plenty of time for that." "Can't be done." "Not today." "It could be dangerous." "What would other people think?" and so on. Most people have picked up these phrases from their own inner saboteurs. But isn't it about time we reduced the influence of this little saboteur, and crossed the invisible border to realize our intentions and promote our personal growth?

The first step is to recognize clearly in which areas of our lives the saboteur keeps playing tricks on us. Experience shows that this varies widely from one person to another, and depends on the fact that our inner saboteurs have very different talents and types of "education". As a result, just like human beings, they have developed specialities. Certainly, all inner saboteurs are active in a number of everyday situations, but almost all—according to the structure and personality of their master or mistress—have one or two main fields of action.

The greatest number of hostile opponents are found in the fields of *health*, *fitness* and *movement*.

**At the saboteurs' festival there are plenty of tempting New Year resolutions**

A seminar participant reported that she had a constant battle with her weight and was getting tired of trying one diet after another. Her doctor had strongly advised her to take up sport. But this was where her little saboteur was most powerful. Despite all her efforts she couldn't overcome her reluctance. Since she was now in the process of reforming her eating habits, even her shopping trips had become an arena for heated discussions with her invisible companion—and quite often he succeeded in tempting her back to pizza, fries and cream cakes. Moreover, he always provided her with countless excuses, even when it was a question of going to see the doctor for her regular health checkups. How much better it would be for her if she could succeed in restraining her inner saboteur in this area!

Other people do battle with their inner saboteurs when it's a question of *undertaking major projects and seeing them through* (whether it's taking an exam, writing a book or preparing a presentation), or *in daily professional life*, not only when necessary risks have to be taken.

A man I interviewed recently on this subject told me that he encountered his inner saboteur in three contexts in his work. The first was when he needed to organize his time and keep to a schedule. He had already attended several time-management seminars, and by then he could probably even have conducted one himself. But focusing himself the evening before to make a plan for the next day was a battle he often lost. His second problem was that his little saboteur often seemed to sit down on top of his pile of papers, employing every possible trick to prevent him from doing the filing. And finally—and this was the most dastardly trick of all—his adversary's seductive excuses always seemed to be deployed when he most needed to be honest and upright in his professional decisions, for example, not to cheat an inexperienced client, to refuse dubious offers or decline to do business "off the record". "Other people do it—why shouldn't you?" was the whisper he would hear in his ear. On such occasions it was often difficult to maintain his integrity.

Some little saboteurs always seem to turn up just when someone is finally trying to *tidy up*—whether it's the basement, the garage or the attic that has been long overdue for a clear-out, desk, cupboards or drawers along with files and folders that need to be put in order, or the never-ending chores in the garden.

I will never forget my own "battle with the garage".

We had been living in our new house for barely three months when so many objects had found their way into the garage that I couldn't get the car in any more—so the car was parked outside and the junk was kept nice and dry. Within a year it was almost impossible to get in there. There was no question about it—the garage must be cleared out, but guess who wasn't keen? My little inner saboteur. He actually succeeded in getting the clearing-out project postponed for another year. Last spring—I had already started writing this book—my wife slyly asked: "Well, are you going to explain to your readers how to deal with the garage saboteur?" Bull's-eye! My saboteur howled in pain. The following Saturday I set to work. And—well, what did you think? By mid-day the job was done. I had made three car journeys to the local rubbish dump. What was left behind was neatly sorted. I had even enjoyed it, and I was very pleased with my own efforts. There was only one question: Why hadn't I done it before?

The "procrastination" saboteur robs us of an immense amount of energy, and the amazing experience of most people is that when you finally get down to the job, it is almost always much easier than you expected, and even very rewarding.

These are probably areas of activity of our little saboteurs in our everyday lives. They keep turning up when it is a question of *trying or learning something new*, whether this is a foreign language, a musical instrument, dancing or using a computer. In my seminars, when we are discussing the fields of activity of the inner saboteur, I often hear stories such as this one:

> Anita, a student of law in Hamburg, had been given a new laptop by her father more than a year earlier, but still didn't really understand how to use it, let alone how to get connected to the internet. For a long time she had wanted to "get in there" and learn how to surf. But the saboteur sitting in front of the computer was getting bigger day by day, and always came up with new excuses.

I encouraged Anita to try writing down all her saboteur's excuses and bring them to the next seminar. What she presented to us was a really interesting collection:

- You don't really need all this new technology—it's just a passing fashion.
- Up to now, you've got on perfectly well without a computer or the internet.
- Handwritten letters are much more personal and elegant. It would be a pity if no one wrote by hand any more.
- The internet is all sex and violence, and you don't know who may be storing your personal details.
- All that flickering is bad for your eyes, and people are already becoming addicted to the web.
- Surely you don't want to become part of this tendency to make everything technological and anonymous?
- Computers and the internet are not for creative people like you,

who enjoy personal contact.

- Anyway, you should be taking a proper computer course; if you made a mistake, the thing could crash and you could lose all your data. That can't happen with handwritten records.
- Better wait a bit—technology is developing so fast, in a year's time it will all get much easier. So just take your time.

These excuses were familiar to most of the other seminar participants. furthermore, they also come up in seminars on other subjects. As you will discover in Part II, the inner saboteurs have been trained in a similar way on their own further education courses ...

And where else does this little enemy appear? For many people, it's when they have to *make important decisions*: in their careers, in their relationships with their partners or even when moving house. Here too, the inner saboteur is at work as a "procrastination specialist". Just as in *contacts with others*: he stops us from writing important letters, or making unpleasant phone calls; he causes us to delay accepting invitations or planned visits, and to promptly forget to return borrowed objects.

If *the courage of one's convictions* is called for, he becomes particularly active. He doesn't like us to take sides in a public discussion; he is too concerned about burning his fingers. He is anxious to save his own skin, too, when we incur possible risk as a result of being too honest in family circles, with our partners or among our friends. Better to keep your trap shut—that's his motto.

Here's another favorite area of activity for your little adversary—he likes to interfere at times when we want to acquire some "cultural input" or polish up our education. Without fail, he will wreck any such plans. It's all too easy for him to make himself comfortable in front of the television and hide that book you were finally going to get around to reading.

And he can even stop us *doing nothing*! Some people have real difficulty in making time to meditate regularly, to take breaks in the course of their working day. And not only then—some people have problems with their inner saboteur when they actually want to do nothing at all.

> I remember a man who was simply bursting with energy. He had no problems with willpower and had attained all the goals of his life. There was no challenge to which he was not equal. At the seminar he attended, participants were asked to take part in a so-called saboteur exercise by the following day, by confronting one's own inner saboteur in some way. At first he seemed rather at a loss. Next morning, everyone was wondering what sort of challenge he had posed himself. With a rather hesitant smile, he said he had done nothing— that had been the most difficult thing he could think of, managing to do nothing while everyone else was doing something. This was when he encountered his inner saboteur.

This seminar participant is certainly not the only person who needs to exercise his willpower in order to do nothing at all, just for once!

So, these are the most important *fields of activity* that have been established in research into inner saboteurs. But this is certainly not a conclusive view of the areas affected by these strange creatures. They will also come into play in any context where one must *pull oneself together and exercise willpower to progress further, or needs to confront a challenge.*

The following summary shows the most frequent areas of activity of the inner saboteur. Using the checklist on page 24 you can then establish the *activity profile of your own personal saboteur: where* in everyday life you will encounter him, and *how strongly* he will influence you. In this way, you will not only become more

**Give yourself and your little saboteur a break from time to time!**

aware of the areas in which you are most vulnerable to the attacks of the little saboteur, but also of things that are *not* difficult for you but are, in fact, a struggle for others.

| Where the saboteur rules | |
| --- | --- |
| **Area** | **In particular** |
| ❶ Health and nutrition | • Health checks by your doctor<br>• Healthy nutrition, weight loss<br>• Giving up unhealthy habits |
| ❷ Fitness and exercise | • Regular exercise such as jogging, going to the gym and other sport<br>• Using the car less |
| ❸ In the workplace | • Planning your time effectively<br>• Eliminating the backlog<br>• Honesty and integrity<br>• Further education and training |
| ❹ Completing projects | • Training<br>• Preparation for examinations<br>• Final examinations and completion of studies<br>• Presentations |
| ❺ Tackling and learning new subjects | • Using computers and the internet<br>• Dance class<br>• Musical instrument<br>• Foreign language |
| ❻ Keeping the home clean and tidy | • Basement, attic and garage<br>• Gardening<br>• Ironing<br>• Desk, drawers, cupboards<br>• Files and folders |
| ❼ Making important decisions | • Choosing or changing your job<br>• Moving house<br>• In relationships and with partners |

| Where the saboteur rules (continued) | |
| --- | --- |
| **Area** | **In particular** |
| ⑧ Contacts with others | • Important letters and telephone calls<br>• Invitations and visits to be returned<br>• Returning borrowed items<br>• Honesty with family, friends and partner |
| ⑨ Having the courage of your convictions | • Publicly taking sides on behalf of a person or party<br>• Making a speech<br>• Involvement in politics, society and the environment |
| ⑩ Cultural activities | • Reading more books, watching less television<br>• Going to the theater, concerts, lectures and exhibitions<br>• Taking stock and resting |
| ⑪ Taking stock and inward contemplation | • Meditation<br>• Moments of reflection<br>• Sometimes just doing nothing |
| ⑫ General | • Any situation in which we need to exercise willpower, or need to confront danger |

## Activity profile of my personal little saboteur

On which occasions do I most frequently encounter my little saboteur, and where does he cause me most trouble?

| Activity/project | Saboteur activity level | | | | | |
| --- | --- | --- | --- | --- | --- | --- |
| | Low | | | | | High |
| | 1 | 2 | 3 | 4 | 5 | 6 |
| Tidying | | | | | | |
| Gardening | | | | | | |
| Dealing with finances | | | | | | |
| Tax return | | | | | | |
| Getting up earlier | | | | | | |
| Sport, such as jogging, going to the gym | | | | | | |
| Healthier eating habits | | | | | | |
| Dieting, weight loss | | | | | | |
| Health checks at doctor's surgery | | | | | | |
| Writing or replying to letters | | | | | | |
| Unpleasant telephone calls | | | | | | |
| Delayed visits and invitations | | | | | | |
| Computers and the internet | | | | | | |
| Dance class, language course, musical instrument | | | | | | |
| Reading books | | | | | | |
| Concerts, theater, exhibitions | | | | | | |
| Watching less television | | | | | | |
| Getting to grips with major work projects | | | | | | |
| Career decisions | | | | | | |
| Clarifying relationship issues | | | | | | |
| Discussions with children or parents | | | | | | |
| Moving house | | | | | | |
| Travel, postponed or delayed | | | | | | |
| Confronting a personal challenge | | | | | | |
| Giving a talk | | | | | | |
| Expressing possibly unpopular opinion or taking sides | | | | | | |
| Showing myself as I am (with my weaknesses) | | | | | | |
| Taking stock, meditation | | | | | | |
| Just doing nothing once in a while | | | | | | |
| | | | | | | |
| | | | | | | |
| | | | | | | |

Now, enter your saboteur's five most important areas of activity in the table below. In this way you will be clearly reminded of where you most often encounter him.

| The five most important areas of activity of my little saboteur |
| --- |
| **1** |
| **2** |
| **3** |
| **4** |
| **5** |

The next step is to establish what methods saboteurs use in general, and your own in particular. Part II of this book will provides comprehensive insights into the box of tricks used by these charlatans.

# PART II

# TRICKS AND TACTICS OF THE LITTLE SABOTEUR

In a huge cave in a secret place, far away from civilization, lies the school for saboteurs—or at least, so we are told by a number of leading researchers in the field. While their prospective masters and mistresses are still in their infancy, this is where the young saboteurs are being trained as meticulously as secret agents. Here they learn not only all sorts of tricks and tactics, but also how to work "underground", that is, largely unobserved. One of the basic principles of their training is:

**As long as no one notices you,
you can work undisturbed.**

And this is something that little saboteurs, with their superlative camouflage techniques, seem to have mastered to a remarkable degree. Most people realize only after the event that they were "prevented" from completing a project or bringing themselves to do something difficult. Almost always, they become conscious of their inner saboteur only when he has already "struck", for example, successfully wrecked a good intention. Many adults, if you ask them about their little saboteurs, will admit, yes, they have one (hasn't everyone?)—but it's seldom that they are actually aware of them.

Is this theory about the school for saboteurs really true, or is it all just a fantasy? Who knows? There is some evidence for its existence, because one thing is certain: the little saboteur is one of the most sophisticated secret agents around. How is it possible for intelligent adults such as ourselves to allow ourselves to be tricked in this way without even noticing? There are *two main causes*:

- We have already got so *used* to our inner saboteurs that we *automatically* delay or forget to do things, often without even noticing.
- Saboteurs are *masters of disguise* and are amazingly skilled at keeping themselves hidden. We can't even smell them. (We only

notice the nasty smell of their success!) But above all they are highly intelligent and creative in the production of *excuses*, particularly those using the favorite formula, "Yes, but ..." It can often be like the famous race between the hare and the tortoise: the little saboteur, with his objections and excuses, always seems to get there first!

If we want to put an end to this situation and stop allowing ourselves to be sabotaged, the first decisive step to take is to *get to know* the various *tricks and tactics* of our inner saboteur. Then we will more easily notice him when, yet again, he attempts to interfere with our plans. What chance do we have against an invisible opponent? Only when we know where he is standing, and what tricks he is likely to use, is it possible to stand up to him effectively.

Our little saboteur may attempt to wreck our plans *at different points in time*:

- He may hinder our decisions in advance.
- He may make sure that the decision itself appears questionable.
- And if he has still not been successful, he will change tack and sabotage the execution of the plan, so as to cloud our judgement after the event and comfortingly lull our suspicions every time a germ of doubt manifests itself.

The school for saboteurs: this is where they learn their crafty tricks

# 1
# THE BLOCKED DECISION

Our little saboteur prefers to use preventive measures. He digs deep into his box of tricks in order to nip in the bud any potential decisions that might have anything to do with exerting willpower, attacking a long-deferred project or changing one's habits for the better. As long as we move along our familiar track and encounter no new situations, he seems to enjoy a peaceful sleep. In this way he often gets completely forgotten in our daily lives. But at the first sign that we are thinking of conquering new territory, making some change in our lives, his alarm bell starts to ring. Instantly he is wide awake. And straight away he starts pulling out all the stops to induce us to abandon our budding plans as quickly as possible. There seem to be no limits to his imagination. And the problem here is: *The more intelligent the human being, the more imaginative is his inner saboteur!*

Here are his favorite "bestsellers" from his box of tricks, spiced with the 20 principles from the saboteurs' manual:

**A saboteur's box of tricks is almost inexhaustible**

## IMPOSSIBILITY TACTICS

For a long time, my cousin Marion had had her annual tax return prepared by her father. After his death, she considered taking charge of this herself, to save the expense of employing an accountant. Her friends who looked after their own tax affairs encouraged her in her decision. It wasn't so difficult and she could do it in a weekend, "no problem". "Well, let's see, I'll have a look at it all and then decide." The following Saturday she went to her desk and got busy with the documents and files containing her tax papers. But in no time at all, on looking through the complex documents and piles of unsorted receipts, she came to a clear realization: "Impossible! How is one supposed to cope with all this? I can't make head nor tail of it. I'll never manage it!" Almost in relief, she put all the papers away again and arranged to meet her friend Robert. When she had convinced him too that she was incapable of mastering the job, the decision had already been made as to who would prepare the tax return for her … Meanwhile her little saboteur grinned in satisfaction, while nibbling at her cream cake, as a sort of reward for wrecking her good resolution.

Principle No. 1
**Belief in the impossibility of the enterprise prevents the moving of mountains!**

Attempting the impossible is a waste of time—everyone knows that. This is why our little saboteur likes to come trotting along with the suggestion that you simply regard the plan as impossible to carry out. He likes most of all to serve up universally applicable "impossibility formulas", such as:

- "It can't be done."
- "No one could be expected to do that."
- "It's an insoluble problem."
- "It just won't work!"
- "That's much too difficult."

These excuses absolve us from all obligation to act; in fact, logically, we need not even make the required decision. As the wise ancient Romans used to say, "Impossibilium nulla est obligatio" (there is no obligation to do something impossible). So why not follow the ancient wisdom—and not even try? Because if no one can do it, I certainly can't be expected to do it. And even if, despite this attitude, we should make the attempt, our own personal saboteur will prove to us beyond doubt that he was right all along.

"I can't do it" is a typical excuse put into our heads by the little saboteur. He is particularly fond of the absolutism of the *prognosis for the future*: "I'll never manage that!" No wonder we refuse to abandon our cosy mental cubbyhole if the prospect is permanent bad weather. The empirical variant on this statement is: "I tried it before, and it didn't work." ("I always knew it wouldn't.")

And if, sometimes, it doesn't seem quite impossible, it also seems equally unreasonable to undertake something that "isn't worth it" or "doesn't make sense". Many people throw in the towel in advance, just to prove to themselves the senselessness of the plan (this is technically known as a "self-fulfilling prophecy"). And, *the more pessimistic your attitude to life, the more frequently you are likely to use this sort of "impossibility" formula.*

In reality, this cleverly disguised excuse means "I don't want to!", "I daren't" or "I'm comfortable with the way things are". (Further "aids to translation" can be found in Part III, from page 111.)

But, you could object at this point, there are some things that really *are* impossible! Well, of course there are, but these are not what we are talking about here. What we have in mind are the many good intentions which *in themselves* could quite possibly be carried out, if we didn't allow our inner saboteur to convince us in advance of their "impossibility". And if we are honest with ourselves, we know perfectly well which these are.

A crafty variant of the "impossibility" tactic is the very common *pseudo-impossibility* version: "no time". How often, and how quickly, in everyday life a plan or a wish is declined with the statement that, unfortunately, "I just haven't the time."

"Could you possibly help me move house this weekend?" someone asks his friend. "Oh, I'd have been glad to, really, but unfortunately I just don't have time." (What a pity! When he would really have loved to help!) "I really ought to take a few days off soon, to relax, have a holiday," a colleague recently said to me, "but I simply can't even consider it, I just don't have the time." (What bad luck that the universe hasn't put more time at our disposal!) And a tradesman who had agreed to carry out a repair for us and failed to turn up on the appointed day made the simple excuse: "I had so much to do, I simply didn't get around to it. Sorry, no time!" (Yes, I'm sorry too. But what can you do? Of course I understand, he just didn't have time ...!)

Isn't it crazy that nearly all of us keep using this excuse and accepting it from others, although it's quite clear that it's not true? For after all, everyone has time. Everyone has 24 hours every day. You only have to take them (not from others, but from your own budget), and use them in a sensible way. Because, particularly in today's fast-paced world, time is a precious possession that needs to be carefully handled. All we mean by saying "I don't have time" is that we are simply giving priority to other things. *So when anyone says he hasn't got time, what he really means is that other things are more important to him.*

But instead of saying this plainly, it seems to be easier to make pressure of time into the scapegoat. At any rate, it's easier for our little saboteur—and he likes to make time to keep playing that joker card, the excuse about not having time.

In this world of chronic shortage of time, maybe people should start to be more aware of how they handle time. Would you like to be with someone who is always trying to make use of you, battle against you or even kill you? Most people try to "make use" of the time they have as best they can, "battle against" time when they are in a hurry, or even "kill" time during their leisure hours. As a result, they find themselves with very little spare time. Think about it:

### "No time!"

Many people complain that they have *no time*,
But they have enough time.
But they had to *pass the time*,
And afterwards they complained
That someone had *wasted their time*
And after that, they were suspicious of anyone
Who claimed to *have time*.

Wrong! Everyone has *enough time*!
You just have to *take* it.
But make no mistake:
Not from other people.
The only person from whom you can *take time*
Is yourself.
And then you must *be careful* with your time
And not *waste* it yet again,
Otherwise you will be right after all:
You have no time!

## THE GAME OF THE MAGIC HAT

*Consideration, a sense of duty* and *morality* are three of the most popular "magic hats" used by the little saboteur. Wearing these disguises, they are socially acceptable. These hats even have honorable status, and so we tend to wear them with pride.

Some time ago I was told the following story by a man who came to one of my seminars:

> The nursery school attended by his two children was organizing a fancy-dress party. The parents were asked to join in the fun and perform a party piece, to make things go with a swing. The father in question thought it was a good idea, but he was shy about appearing in public, especially if he had to dress up for the occasion. The day of the party drew near, the children's excitement grew—but so did the resistance of his inner saboteur. On the one hand he didn't want to disappoint his children, but on the other hand he was hoping to be able to get out of the whole thing. Then he was "saved" by an important appointment. Duty called—and surely everyone would understand. Everyone except his children; they were bitterly disappointed that—once again—their daddy was the only one not to join in.

Principle No. 2
**When duty calls, many a good
resolution falls by the wayside.**

In our social circles, *following the path of duty* is almost blindly accepted, even respected. Whatever you do is fine, as long as you do your duty. How many actions have been justified by the excuse that you were "only doing your duty"! But when our little saboteur chooses to suggest this form of justification to us, we ourselves are the victims. We deny ourselves a longed-for trip, membership of a gym or the time we so desperately need for ourselves or our family, because our commitments allegedly allow no time for them. The decision to do something, at last, for our private life and wellbeing is buried behind the excuse of having one's duty to fulfil.

The successful author Reinhard Sprenger puts it very aptly in his book *Die entscheidung liegt bei Dir! Wege aus der taglichen Unzufriedenheit* [*The Decision is Yours! How to Deal with Everyday Dissatisfaction*]: "Duty often makes its appearance in the grey sackcloth of self-denial, accompanied by an aura of self-sacrifice. [...] Duty is often an excuse, because it saves [many people] the task of defining their own aims and making unpalatable decisions. They avoid jumping in at the deep end because of the need to fulfil their duty."

It must have been that little saboteur on the bank who put up the sign reading "No diving"!

And how many important actions remain unexecuted out of *false consideration for others*! Perhaps you know this well-known story:

An elderly couple discover one morning, at breakfast in the old people's home, that the husband actually prefers the bottom half of the bread roll, and his wife the top half. But out of mistaken consideration, in order to please him, the wife had always passed the top half to her husband. And he had always eaten it up like a good boy, believing that she preferred the bottom half of the roll. As a result of this misunderstanding, they had lived together for 45 years, each allowing the other the wrong half of the roll!

Principle No. 3
**Consideration for others absolves you
from taking responsibility.**

Many inner saboteurs cunningly appeal to our consideration for others. They are very concerned that we should *spare the feelings of others*, *do right* by them. They want us to please other people! So we prefer not to express our own needs, and would rather suffer in silence instead of talking about it: "I can't do that to him!" "I can't burden her with that!" After all, we could run the risk of forfeiting the approval of our fellow human beings.

Perhaps we are just being cowardly? Perhaps! But that's exactly the trick—hiding our anxiety under the "magic hat" of consideration for others.

In some cases, even *morality* may be invoked. Nothing wrong with a system of values, a basic ethical attitude that aims to improve your own life and that of other people. But inner saboteurs often hide behind a morality that *limits your life*, which is based on what is "done" and what is "proper behavior". Just when you feel the urge to express warmth, helpfulness and spontaneity (something similar to the courage of your convictions), you may hear an inner voice: "People don't do that sort of thing! Don't get involved!"

I will never forget the couple, no longer young, who lived in the flat below us at our last address. These two were always at loggerheads. It was impossible to ignore their frequent arguments, yelling, banging of doors, and loud weeping. One evening the wife fled for refuge to our flat, because her rows with her husband were once again threatening to become physically violent. She told us her story.

She had never loved her husband. And she would never have married him if it had not been for the conventional attitude of her family. When she found herself pregnant by him, there seemed to be absolutely no solution except to get married. Her strictly religious background, in a small village,

**You'd like the top half? It's a pleasure!**

put pressure on her to "correct her mistake" as quickly as possible. Even her own mother had associated herself with "public opinion", although she knew that her prospective son-in-law was prone to violence. By now, the child had become an adult. Divorce? No, she couldn't possibly do that to her parents!

That evening, I was deeply dismayed by the activities of the inner saboteurs who had here concealed themselves behind the cloak of morality. But when I began to consider whether I shouldn't have a word with the husband (as the wife had asked me to do), my own inner saboteur swung into action. For although part of me was inclined to support my neighbor, the little saboteur successfully switched on all the warning lights. "It wouldn't be appropriate to interfere," he said in persuasive tones, "even if you would like to help. In fact, no one should ever get involved in other people's affairs. It's simply not done!"

The admonition "it's simply not done" was one that even the disciples of Jesus encountered from the lips of the Pharisees, when they dared to pick ears of corn on the Sabbath, because they were hungry. The saying of Jesus that all moral principles should serve mankind, and not the other way around, has been too often overlooked in the Christian West, and this is still the case today.

We need not go more deeply into the question of how many actions remain unexecuted day after day because of moral misunderstandings, or how many negative deeds, on the other hand, have been carried out under the cloak of morality. Only a glance at recent history suffices—and this probably also applies to our own lives.

# THE LANGUAGE OF NON-COMMITMENT

"Well, have you made any New Year resolutions?" Karen asked her friend Tina, whom she had telephoned on the afternoon of 1 January to compare notes on how they had spent New Year's Eve. Tina replied enthusiastically: "Oh, I think I'd better do more sport, maybe I could start jogging, and also I probably ought to go on a diet some time ..." "Yes, you're right," replied Karen, "actually I ought to cut right down on my smoking, and I ought to work on my relationship with Mark a bit more. Maybe we could do a dance class together, or I could go to the theater with him more often. In fact, I really ought to do more about my cultural life ..." Yes, Tina thought so too, and so they continued to encourage each other about all the ways in which they *really ought to* improve their lives. At the end of the conversation Tina remarked, "Well, perhaps we should get together some time, do something together ..." "Yes, we really ought to do that some time. All right, see you then!" (But when *would* they see each other? the little saboteur thought, laughing to himself.)

The thing is not to be definite, not to commit oneself, because that would mean actually doing something. *Remember*: Inner saboteurs are masters of the *non-committal*, and the language of non-commitment is the *conditional* tense: "I probably ought to ..." "It would be better for me to ..." "Really I shouldn't ..." "Maybe I could try ..." These are the kinds of formulae that make your little enemy's mouth water. The consequences of this "conditioning" are obvious: there won't be any! For "conditional insights" hardly ever result in action, because non-action is already programmed into their non-committal formulation. This is why your personal saboteur likes to allow you to phrase your ideas for improvement in the conditional tense—and then roll over on his side on the sofa with a self-satisfied smirk: no danger of immediate action in sight.

**Principle No. 4**
**Good resolutions formulated in the conditional tense are seldom carried out.**

However, the inner saboteur often reaches the heights of non-commitment by the use of the ominous little word "one" (often in combination with the conditional tense). With these three letters, we surrender all claims to a personal point of view to the "cloakroom of social convention". We don't even notice it, because we already use the word "one" in so many different contexts: "One should ..." "One really ought to ..." "One had better ..." "Perhaps one could ..." Yes, of course one should. But who, may I ask, should or could? "What, me? Oh, no, not at all! You misunderstood me, I did say quite clearly 'one' ..." Result: *"One" is the password to being allowed to remain personally passive.*

As long as this little word is not, exceptionally, being used to describe a generally valid state of affairs (for example, "When in Rome, one should do as the Romans do"), then you can be quite sure that behind it lies a little saboteur who doesn't wish you to express a definite opinion. What do you think? One really ought to give this some thought some time!

## Delaying Tactics

Colin, 33, had been a qualified engineer for seven years, but was still living with his parents. From the day he completed his training, he had been wanting to move into his own apartment—there was no financial obstacle to this, but everything was so much more pleasant at home—after all, his washing was done, his room was cleaned and he even had his meals cooked for him. But he did not consider these to be valid reasons to stay put. First of all, he was not at all sure what part of town he should move to, and then he had to look into the question of whether it was better to rent or buy. But he kept postponing the appointment with his financial adviser. Perhaps it would be better for him to attend a seminar on investment in property, so as to acquire the necessary knowledge about the opportunities and risks of buying an apartment? After he had finally worked out which of the various seminars on this subject was the best one, and, a year later, had actually taken part in one, he came to the conclusion that it was best not to buy just yet, but to invest his money and rent instead. On the other hand, he explained to his friend who asked him expectantly whether he was now going to move into an apartment of his own, on the other hand he ought to consider first of all whether it wouldn't be a better idea to move in with his girlfriend, Susan. This was three years ago. He is still living at home, because first of all he ought to …

We all know them—people who have always wanted to give a talk, write a book, go on a diet or take up some new sport—and have never managed to get around to it. When you ask about it, they say: "I can't do it yet, first I need to …" Of course, the right conditions need to be created first—or, better still, arise of their own accord. Research must be done, a book must be read, a seminar attended, an adviser consulted or a survey carried out. These *delaying tactics* of the inner saboteur express themselves in the well-known disease of *procrastinationitis*. "What can be done today can easily be put off until tomorrow", is the little saboteur's proverb. He is only too happy to put things on the back burner, wagging his tail in the process.

Principle No. 5

**The back burner is the saboteur's
favorite workplace.**

Perfectionists in particular always take refuge behind the please-not-yet-first-I-have-to attitude. "Go ahead just like that? Unthinkable!" "I'm still waiting for official authorization." From whom, may I ask? Of course, from the Ministry of Inner Sabotage! Well, you'll have a long wait. For these little saboteurs like to have an easy life: they shy away from action, would rather debate instead of act, and preferably give the whole scenario a great deal more thought. In any case, in the end it could all turn out to be unnecessary.

## PLAYING IT DOWN

Richard was under great stress at work. When he first began to get heartburn and stomach ache, he ignored it. He refused to give up his coffee. "It's not as bad as all that. I'm not going to let it get me down." But his physical complaints increased, and he rejected his wife's advice to see the doctor, with the words: "It'll go away of its own accord. I've survived worse." After some time he began to get cramp-like attacks in his stomach. Now he gave up coffee, and even willingly drank the camomile tea made for him by his wife, but as for going to the doctor, "plenty of time for that". His colleague Joe told him that he had often had similar problems: "Nothing for a chap to worry about. Don't make a mountain out of a molehill—reactions like that are quite normal when you're under stress at work." Nevertheless, Richard gratefully accepted the stomach tablets Joe offered him. They really did relieve his symptoms to some extent. "I knew it—one doesn't need to bother the doctor over every little thing." But the cramps became more frequent and more painful. One night he woke up in so much pain that he did after all call the emergency doctor, who got him straight into hospital. Diagnosis: perforated gastric ulcer.

## Principle No. 6
### Reassurance is a narcotic which may have crippling side effects.

"It's not that bad!" "Doesn't matter!" "Not that important!" "Other people do it too—so just relax in your armchair and don't worry." A few little complaints, a little brandy, a few cigarettes, that one exception … all these things would appear quite harmless, if it wasn't for the story about the frog:

> A frog was thrown into boiling hot water—and jumped straight out again. Next he was thrown into cold water, which was very gradually brought to the boil. Although he could have jumped out at any time, he stayed in the water—and perished. Because of the slow increase in temperature, he had not noticed the danger.

The interpretation of this story is obvious. It's up to us to recognize what is actually harmless and what apparent trifles can harm us, others or the environment. The inner saboteur is a bad adviser here, since in case of doubt he finds it easier to play the matter down and carry on as usual. The unpleasant awakening comes when the "harmless" incidents add up to lasting damage, or at least a condition that has become difficult to treat. The fact that our accomplices may have turned into companions in misfortune will be seen as very cold comfort. And the inner saboteur? About now, his usual ditty of "it's not all that bad" will no longer be heard, and we will hear his master or mistress whispering the well-known saying: "I thought it wasn't that important, or there was plenty of time!" Too late!

## NOT MY RESPONSIBILITY

Everyone knows the following situations:

> After a long wait in a restaurant (your stomach is rumbling with hunger, and you are about to die of thirst) a waiter finally approaches, but on our signalling to him, we are dished up the following remark: "Not my table—the other waiter will be with you right away."
>
> This is a situation we may also experience with authorities. The lack of someone with the appropriate responsibility means that the expected action may unfortunately not take place. "That's not my job." "Please ask the boss when he comes in." "Mrs X always does that, not me."

**Principle No. 7**
**If it's not your responsibility,**
**you don't have to do anything.**

This is exactly the motto according to which my saboteur operates. Recently, when a professional colleague was in difficulties and I was trying to think how I could help him, a voice in my head said: "This really isn't my business. Why me?" This reaction is certainly human and understandable, but … my little saboteur immediately came up with further justifications: "After all, it's not my fault." "What's it got to do with me?" "It's not my responsibility!" "There must be others who could be of much more help." My saboteur whispered to me: If you are *not responsible*, you can innocently wash your hands of the matter and retain a good conscience. Or can you? Luckily, my colleague's problem continued to prey on my mind. I mentally blocked my ears to fend off my saboteur's diversion tactics, and straight away I realized: "It *does* have something to do with me!"

Oh dear, thought my saboteur, it would have been better not to have known anything about it. After all, what I don't know can't hurt me. This is the heightened version of the not-my-responsibility tactic: the *ostrich tactic*. Just stick your head in the sand! This may work—temporarily—but he who hides his head in the sand today may be gnashing his teeth tomorrow! (After Reinhard K. Sprenger, *Die entscheidung liegt bei Dir! Wege aus der taglichen Unzufriedenheit* [The Decision is Yours! How to Deal with Everyday Dissatisfaction].)

## Traditional Clichés

A management consultant who came to one of my seminars told the following story:

> While still pursuing her course of study in business management, she completed a period of practical training in her father's medium-sized musical instrument factory, which employed 20 staff members. After only two weeks, she suggested restructuring measures to him, which would lead to smoother operation and a 15-percent reduction in costs. But the reaction from all sides was one of doubt and hesitation: "We've never done it that way!" "We've always done it the other way!" "Who does she think she is?" As a result, everything stayed as before. Two years later, when her father employed a firm of business consultants, he was quite astonished to find that they suggested similar measures for

rationalizing the business. Again he protested: "This is unheard-of! Where would we be if ..." But the consultant promptly replied: "Yes, exactly!", adding with a smile: *"Where would we be if everyone said 'where would we be', and no one went to see where we would be if we went there?"*

Not only in business firms, but also in private life, when changes are proposed, our little saboteurs' main object is to see that everything stays the same. They avoid change and new ideas like the plague, and try to prevent them by any means possible—and they mostly succeed, however banal these *traditional clichés* may sound. Remarks such as those in the example above, after all, are very common. They are often employed in serious debate. Otherwise, where would we be?

**Principle No. 8**
**Just don't change anything!**
**Things might be different ...**

## PLAYING IT SAFE

Julia was a talented fashion designer who had worked for a textile firm for five years, in a well-paid job. But she always dreamed of becoming independent. Then one day temptation came in the form of a telephone call. Marina, an Italian friend of hers who was also in the fashion industry and who had recently opened her own studio in Milan, invited her to join her in the business, with the chance of becoming a partner after a year. Her long-awaited opportunity had finally arrived! But immediately her inner saboteur bombarded her with counter-arguments. Should she give up her safe job? Would she be able to learn Italian quickly enough and make contacts in Milan? Would her relationship with her boyfriend survive? He would not be able to join her for at least ten months. And what if the whole thing turned out not to be a financial success? Better not take the risk. Should she really put her familiar surroundings at stake for such a risky enterprise? And so she came to the conclusion: "I'd better leave it." In future years she may perhaps tell her daughter how much she has always regretted not seizing this opportunity. But her little saboteur was simply too strong for her.

### Principle No. 9
### If you don't take risks, you won't make a fool of yourself.

"Better safe than sorry!" is a favorite saying of the little saboteur, and he adds: "You could get your fingers burned." "That could be dangerous." "Just don't take the risk." "… and what if something goes wrong?" "Don't make a fool of yourself!" "Better just leave it." If none of this makes a difference, he brings out his most powerful argument as a trump card: "A bird in the hand is worth two in the bush!" In this way, in the guise of protector, he keeps us from experiencing real life. The bird-in-the-hand principle is only half the story, and has little to do with fulfilment in life. A life conducted without taking risks and without the courage to make the occasional mistake, to come a cropper once in a while, is really not a very exciting life, but leads to increasing inner rigidity.

Of course this doesn't mean that we should throw all precautions out of the window and plunge headlong into daredevil enterprises. Rather, it's a case of always seeking new challenges within the limits of one's capabilities, and taking calculated risks. Of course, your little saboteur will follow close on your heels, but you might even find this enjoyable. (How this is to be managed, you will find out in Part III, from page 97 onwards.)

## THE EASY LIFE

Why didn't Colin in the story earlier pull himself together and leave home? He argued that first of all he had to find out about the pros and cons of buying and renting, but in reality he simply found it more convenient at home, where he didn't have to bother about cooking, cleaning, washing and ironing. Making the break in order to get an apartment together with his girlfriend would probably only mean that once again he would be relieved of these chores.

There is something to be said for an *easy life!* Our saboteur is well aware of this. He likes an easy life too …

Principle No. 10
**If you want to take it easy tomorrow,
you'd better start practising now …**

Sometimes, when nothing else occurs to him, he will try to stop us taking a decision by pointing us towards the comfortable armchair and whispering: "Just sit down and relax." Because one of the little saboteur's favorite spots is the chair in front of the television.

How comforting it is to switch on the box, enjoying vicarious emotions and watching other people taking plunges in life! And the decisive difference is that if we don't like it, we can just switch off. In real life, unfortunately, that's not the case. So many things in our lives fall victim to convenience. So many people drive or take a taxi instead of riding a bicycle; it's easier to ring for a pizza than cook a meal oneself, and plenty of people can be put off a planned climb to a mountain peak when their inner saboteurs draw their attention to the convenient mountain railway. But the most convenient decision of all is not even to make any decision!

The television chair: harmless, and so comfortable!

# 2
# DECISIONS, DECISIONS

The success of an enterprise largely stands or falls by the unambiguous nature of the decision. Our inner saboteur, however, makes every effort to *prevent unambiguous and binding decisions*, since they considerably inhibit his room for maneuver and his sphere of influence. He has various ways to succeed in *watering down a decision*. This almost invariably results in failure.

## TRY AND TRY AGAIN

"I will try to get up at 6 o'clock tomorrow for a change," Thomas announced to his father with a look of sincerity in his eyes. Yes, he did really mean it "quite sincerely". He had every intention of doing so, though normally he did not manage to crawl out of bed before 8am. But "fate" apparently willed otherwise, for next morning he was late again at the breakfast table, reporting with a guilty expression: "I did try, but …" What a pity! But at least he did try!

Principle No. 11
"Trying" costs nothing—
and results in nothing.

Tragically, there is no shortage of professional "triers" these days. They come up with good intentions as though on a production line—and never follow up with action. Anyone who only *tries* to give up smoking, to get to work on time, to clear out the basement, and so on, has little prospect of success. "I did try" is the loser's number-one saying!

Often hidden behind this socially recognized self-deception are a *lack of decisiveness* or an *unwillingness to act*. "I will try", in plain language, usually means "I don't really want to." These little words predispose the enterprise to failure from the start.

"No," the reply is often heard, "I really did want to ..." But the writer Robert Musil would have replied merely: "A wish is an intention that does not take itself seriously!" Or, in other words, anyone who only wants to *try* something leaves the famous *back door* open (for himself and his inner saboteur).

The temptation just to want to try something is great. Incidentally, the sentence from the Lord's Prayer, "And lead us not into temptation", could be understood quite differently, as "And preserve us from the eternal 'just wanting to try'." The answer from heaven would presumably in that case be: "The only person responsible is you yourself. Stop just trying, and say 'I will do ...!'" In this way, you will at least reduce the chances of your personal saboteur wrecking your intentions (you will find out why in Part III, from page 111).

Just to prevent misunderstandings: of course there are situations in life where the expression "to try" fits and is appropriate:

- When one really wants to just *try out or test* something, to find out if it suits.

For example, someone might try for a while to put his work schedule on the computer rather than using a desk diary, but come to the conclusion that it doesn't suit him or her—but not in the sense of "I didn't manage to do it", but in the sense of "I did manage it, but it's not right for me." But it was worth a try!

- When one wants to *express a conscious reservation.*

As Henry is about to leave for work, his wife asks him to buy a new toaster, as the old one is broken. "I'll try" can here actually mean: "I'll do it if at all possible, but I can't be absolutely sure yet if I will be able to get around to it, with all my commitments at work." Then it may happen that a meeting is cancelled, and he has time to go and buy a toaster in his lunch break. However, it could also happen that he originally planned to buy the toaster on his way home, but then unexpectedly had to take over the work of a colleague who was off sick, and couldn't leave the office until 8.15pm.

In both these cases it's not a question of "trying" in the saboteur's sense, which is just a way of watering down a decision!

## SMOKE-SCREEN TACTICS

Why do so many New Year resolutions turn into so much waste paper by the middle of January? At the turn of the year, they were certainly meant very seriously. But unfortunately, when making the decision, the way our brains work was not taken into account. Our control center, like a mail-order firm, can only carry out specific commands. This sort of method just doesn't work:

David places an order with a mail-order firm, asking for "something nice to wear, a few good books, the latest techno- logical gadgets and a few amusing joke items"—and complains later that "these people" haven't delivered the goods!

This is just how we treat our control center, the brain. We make vaguely formulated resolutions to "eat more healthily", "live with greater awareness", "bring up the children in a more consistent manner", "make more time for the family", "do more sport", "lose a lot of weight", "be more careful about spending money", or "earn more". The result: this order can't be delivered! The "team" in your inner control center is in despair—they *want* to help you realize your projects, but they *can't*! They are wandering around in the fog of your vague formulations. Because what most people who try to "place these orders" don't take into account are the brain's "implementation preconditions". The logical effect of these is a further saboteur's principle:

**Principle No. 12**
**Commands phrased as comparatives**
**can't be carried out!**

Our inner saboteurs are masters of the smoke-screen tactic. And when you formulate your aims in such a vague manner, using comparative terms such as "more" or "better", your personal saboteur laughs up his sleeve (or would if he had any sleeves), and looks forward to wrecking your new resolutions yet again. (You will learn in Part III how to formulate your aims in such a way that your saboteur can't wreck them any more, from page 140.)

By the way, smoke screens create not only *comparative formulations*, but also those popular imprecise indications of time such as "some time", "soon" or "in the near future". But more on this soon.

## THE FREE SPIRIT

A few years ago, when we were discussing the topic of scheduling in one of my seminars, one of the participants vehemently declared that she hated planning. Planning was the death of all spontaneity and creativity. The planned economy of the Communist countries had surely proved this. *Free spirits* and *creative people* should not be constrained by plans! Duty rosters were for civil servants and assembly-line workers. But in fact, the situation is somewhat different.

### Principle No. 13
### No deadline—no action!

Your inner saboteur avoids action (he's a lazy character), so he tries with all his strength to prevent anything remotely resembling a *deadline*. He keeps whispering in your ear that a creative person doesn't need any regulations.

But this is a serious mistake when it's a question of decisions that have any prospect of a successful outcome. *Without planning and deadlines you are leaving the realization of your intentions to chance—and chance hardly ever cares about realization!*

The freer your spirit, the less likely it is that you will "spontaneously" carry out your project, particularly in the case of a major project or a lasting change of behavior. Your little saboteur knows this, and will try all possible means to prevent a specific plan. (You can find out how to counteract him successfully in Part III, from page 140.)

## GOODBYE HERCULES!

When William came back from a motivational seminar, he announced that he was going to make radical changes to his life from now on. From tomorrow he would do an hour's sport a day, give up smoking, lose 30lbs, clear out the whole house, keep a daily diary and at last carry out his long-held intention of learning Spanish. The family were amazed. Dad had been transformed into a real Hercules. His little saboteur was amazed too. But he wasn't worried. He knew in advance that he wouldn't even have to do anything. With all these good resolutions, William would be personally responsible for failing to carry them out. And in fact, within a week he was quite his old self again. Well, that's how it goes, his little companion laughed wisely to himself. He'd seen it all before.

**Principle No. 14**
**If you're too ambitious,**
**you won't achieve much.**

"I'm really going to put myself to the test now!" "I'm going to get right down to it!" "You just watch, now I'm really going to show them all what I'm made of!" "I'm really going to sort my life out now." These are all old, well-known phrases that everyone has probably uttered at some time or other—probably out of deep inner conviction, full of thirst for action! Perhaps you were really bursting with enthusiasm, and just couldn't wait to begin. Everything felt right: the clear decision, a precisely-formulated and well-planned aim—and yet, after a short time, you resigned yourself to giving up. Why? Quite simply, *if you take on too much, you may often achieve nothing.*

In the enthusiasm of the moment, we may sometimes feel like Hercules, but the Ancient Greeks already knew how important *realistic* planning is, planning that takes account of everyday circumstances and unforeseen difficulties. Don't be deceived: your saboteur won't deter you from Herculean plans. On the contrary, he will even spur you on, since he knows from experience that the more you undertake, the sooner you will fail. Then of course he will generously come to your rescue.

## Why have the following good intentions little chance of realization?

- "From tomorrow, I shall start walking five miles a day."
- "I probably ought to see the doctor some time."
- "From tomorrow, I'll do everything differently."
- "I ought to eat more healthily!"
- "Soon I'll get around to clearing out the basement."
- "Maybe I could start jogging."
- "Next year I'm going to lose 40 pounds, eat only organic food, stop smoking, start meditating for an hour every day, and do at least an hour's sport every day."
- "I should really cut down on my smoking."
- "I'd like to have more time for my family and children."
- "I ought to eat more fruit."
- "I'm going to live more economically."
- "I really must repot the flowers some time."
- "Maybe I should try to do a bit more sport."

| Why the following good intentions have little chance of realization | |
| --- | --- |
| • "From tomorrow, I shall start walking five miles a day." | Too much to start with, if you are not a regular walker (overtaxing yourself). |
| • "I probably ought to see the doctor some time." | "Probably ought" is doubly non-committal. |
| • "From tomorrow, I'll do everything differently." | "Everything differently" is not specific, and anyway is too much to ask (overtaxing yourself). |
| • "I ought to eat more healthily!" | Non-committal and comparative (not specific). |
| • "Soon I'll get around to clearing out the basement." | "Soon"—no precise time is stated. |
| • "Maybe I could start jogging." | "Maybe" and "could" are non-committal; "jogging" is not specific (for how long, or how far?). |
| • "Next year I'm going to lose 40 pounds, eat only organic food, stop smoking, start meditating for an hour every day, and do at least an hour's sport every day." | Hercules sends his regards (much too much!). |
| • "I should really cut down on my smoking." | "Should really"—no clear decision; "cut down" (by how much?). |
| • "I'd like to have more time for my family and children." | "More time"—comparative, not specific. |
| • "I ought to eat more fruit." | "Ought" is non-committal; "more fruit" is comparative, not specific. |
| • "I'm going to live more economically." | "More economically"—comparative, not specific. |
| • "I really must repot the flowers some time." | "Must" indicates necessity, but "some time" is not specific as to when. |
| • "Maybe I should try to do a bit more sport." | "Maybe"—no clear decision; "should" is non-committal; "try" leaves the back door open; "a bit more"—comparative, not specific. |

# 3
## Sabotaging the Action

Your little saboteur may slowly be getting a bit nervous. If he has not succeeded so far in preventing your decision to take action, or watering down the decision itself, it will now be high time for him to abandon his cosy nest and pull out all the stops that still remain to him. Because now we are coming to the crunch: you are taking action. Or at least you are on the point of taking action. At the same time, he knows that he still has a number of options open to him. He will try to *divert your attention*, to lure you into the *exception trap*, to induce you to *abandon* your action, or in an ominous move to persuade you to *make comparisons with other people* ... until once again you knuckle under to him. Or perhaps not, because by now you are able to see through his tricks.

## Diversionary Tactics

Gabrielle had kept the whole of Saturday free in order to prepare a presentation at the marketing firm where she worked. On this glorious winter day her boyfriend Jack was not very happy about going skiing on his own, but he knew how important this presentation was for Gabrielle's career. He could not have been more understanding about it.

That Saturday morning, Gabrielle got up early, went jogging and then allowed herself a relaxed breakfast to get herself going. But after that, as she still wasn't quite in the right mood, she allowed herself some time to read the Saturday paper (of course, there was always more to read on Saturday). Among the film listings she noticed an old Edgar Wallace film that Jack had long wanted to see, and decided to book tickets for it. After all, you never knew when you would get another chance to see it. "Right, now it really is time to get on with my presentation", she said to herself after ringing up the cinema box office. A glance at the clock revealed how right she was—it was 10.35am already. As she went into her office, she started to think about her presentation and everything that depended on it, and a strange feeling of unease came over her: "Am I really up to the job?" "Do I even have enough specialist knowledge?" "Will my cynical colleagues take the opportunity to tear me to pieces yet again?" No, while she was in this mood she really couldn't start on her work—and certainly not in the chaos that reigned in her office. "Tidying up helps to put your thoughts in order", she had read somewhere recently. So first of all she began to tidy her desk, and then the whole room—after which, of course, she had to get out the vacuum cleaner. Before she knew it, she had undertaken a thorough cleaning of the flat, including washing the dishes and taking out the rubbish. She surveyed her work with satisfaction and, to be honest, she was even rather proud of herself, because tidying up and housework were not usually "her thing".

But her pleasure didn't last long, when she realized that it was actually 1.20pm. "Oh Lord, the presentation!" She began to panic, but calmed herself with the thought that she still had

"the whole day". "Right, here we go!" She had not been sitting at her desk for five minutes and had just sorted out her documents when she became aware that it was Saturday and the shops closed at 2pm. Without a moment's hesitation she went off to buy the food she still needed for the weekend. Meanwhile she resolved to prepare Jack's favorite meal for him that evening, in gratitude for his understanding. She felt a slight twinge as she thought about her boyfriend enjoying himself in the snow and sunshine without her in this beautiful weather. And only so that she could prepare her stupid presentation! And so far she had done precisely nothing! Better get moving! "To save time", she went to the café around the corner for a quick bowl of soup, and because her colleague Maureen happened to be sitting there, she had "just a quick" cup of coffee with her, accompanied by a nice piece of chocolate cake. She was aware that she was temporarily abandoning her diet, because on days like these "one can't fight two battles at once". By about 2.30pm she had explained her plans about the presentation to Maureen, along with all the possible consequences. That had to be helpful, she thought to herself, because she was mentally getting herself in the right frame of mind for work. Maureen thought her ideas were "brilliant" and was sure that she would give a "super performance".

Gabrielle was no longer quite so sure, when by about 3pm she was at last back at her desk, feeling slightly exhausted (why on earth?). Slowly, self-doubt began to gnaw at her. What an undisciplined sort of person she must be, not to have managed to get going with her presentation all day! And had she really done enough research? In order to reassure herself she decided to search for more information about her subject

**He always creeps in again through the back door**

on the internet. Maybe she could come up with some exciting ideas that way. By 4.45pm she was so exhausted from surfing the net and the flickering of her computer screen that she decided to lie down for half an hour. But she fell deeply asleep, and when she woke up an hour later, her limbs felt as heavy as lead. Even a cold shower only partly got her moving again. The presentation? No, today simply was not the right day. In two hours Jack would arrive, and after all she wanted to surprise him with his favorite meal! As a reward for the fact that she had not been able to go with him today—and probably wouldn't be able to do so tomorrow either ... To reverse the well-known proverb, "What you can't do today, just postpone until tomorrow!"

The only person to be happy that day was Gabrielle's saboteur, who had achieved victory right down the line. And since she had not even noticed how he had trained her, the chances were very good that things would go much the same way the next day! Gabrielle finally completed her presentation, under increasing pressure and with a bad conscience, in two night-shifts just before the day she was due to deliver it. "Next time," she swore to herself, "I'll start earlier!" "Well, we'll see," grunted her little saboteur with a confident smirk, nestling comfortably in his basket ...

### Principle No. 15
**Distraction is the first step on the road to failure to achieve one's goal.**

Marvellous, isn't it? Just when you have a clear target, reserve a whole day or longer to achieve it, and just when you are about to start, your inner saboteur goes berserk, although we usually don't notice it. He deploys all his creative powers to prevent our making a start, and seizes upon the subtlest and most effective means of sabotage. Amazingly, he succeeds again and again in inducing an intelligent human being, in broad daylight, to do exactly the opposite of what he or she intended, and moreover, spontaneously, without any external force or pressure. Unbelievable! And not only in broad daylight, but in full possession of his or her mental powers and in full awareness of this intelligent being's *actual* intentions. And yet many a member of the species is actually so naïve as to believe that their *time has been stolen*, that it was somehow *lost* or perhaps *run through their fingers*. Even the little saboteur can hardly believe that much naïveté, but he has given up worrying his head about it. After intensive discussion with his colleagues he has come to the conclusion that the human species is simply prone to inexplicable phenomena, and that's as it should be.

The story of Gabrielle may appear contrived, but only in the choice of persons and context, not in view of the *psychological dynamic of the diversionary tactic*, which works in a very similar way for many people. What actually happened there? Let's look at a sort of X-ray view of the process:

1. Someone has a *major and important project which involves some difficulty for him or her* (for example, to clear out the house, prepare a seminar, talk or presentation, complete a tax return, write an article, book or very important letter, study for an exam, do proof corrections, etc.). This person has set aside a day (or longer) to carry out this project.

2. When it is time to begin, even the *thought of the difficulty* of the work, or of the possibility that it may not be successful, creates *feelings of distress* (or even fear).

3. Almost automatically, the result is the *impulse to avoid* the project (which is associated with negative feelings) and allow oneself to be distracted from it.

4. This (often insidiously tempting) impulse is followed (mostly unconsciously), and *spontaneously changes into less demanding* (often also less important) *or more pleasant occupations*—inwardly accompanied by pseudo-justifications (such as "not being in the right mood" or "just quickly" doing, or even "having to do", something or other.

5. The *briefly-experienced relief* usually quickly turns to *renewed, mostly stronger, negative feelings* (on account of increasing pressure of time and a bad conscience).

6. This again *strengthens the impulse to avoid* and seek distraction once again.

7. The resulting vicious circle can repeat itself until *the project is completely abandoned* or finally completed *right at the last minute* in a "work marathon".

8. The more frequently this process is repeated, the more it *undermines our self-confidence* and thus the greater is the *danger that it will become a habit.*

The diagram opposite graphically demonstrates the course of this diversionary tactic. And what we prefer to be distracted by, you will see from the summary on page 70.

On closer inspection we can discern two points from which we can recognize particularly well how our invisible enemy leads us on to the thin ice: it's a question of fairy tales as well as of seduction and betrayal.

## The fairy tale of the right mood

It's not only children who love fairy tales. Adults, too, allow themselves to be told fairy tales—by their inner saboteur. And one

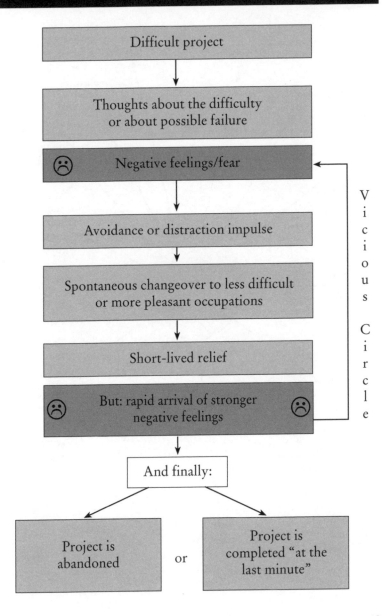

**Diversion procedures**

Difficult project

↓

Thoughts about the difficulty
or about possible failure

↓

☹ Negative feelings/fear

↓

Avoidance or distraction impulse

↓

Spontaneous changeover to less difficult
or more pleasant occupations

↓

Short-lived relief

↓

☹ But: rapid arrival of stronger
negative feelings ☹

↓

And finally:

↙          ↘

Project is
abandoned          or          Project is
completed "at the
last minute"

V
i
c
i
o
u
s

C
i
r
c
l
e

## Favorite diversionary maneuvers

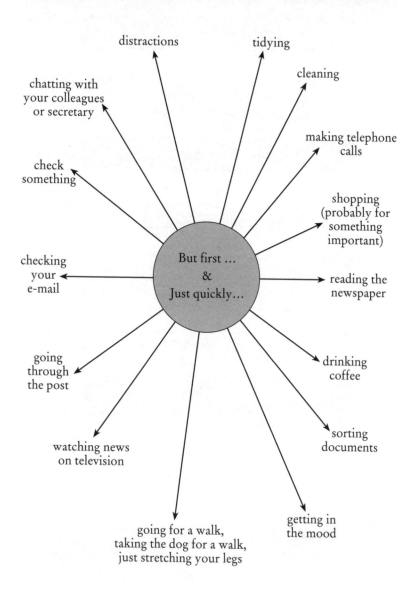

distractions

tidying

cleaning

chatting with
your colleagues
or secretary

making telephone
calls

check
something

shopping
(probably for
something
important)

checking
your
e-mail

But first …
&
Just quickly…

reading the
newspaper

going
through
the post

drinking
coffee

watching news
on television

sorting
documents

going for a walk,
taking the dog for a walk,
just stretching your legs

getting in
the mood

of his favorites is the *fairy tale of the right (or wrong) mood*. Most people believe this fairy tale in the initial phase of a new project, when they think they always need to be *inspired* or *in the right mood* to be able to begin. "I'm really not in the right mood yet," they say to themselves or others, "I'm just not feeling motivated." Oh, what a pity! But if we look at this attitude quite soberly, it reveals itself as an ominous illusion: *"I'm not motivated"* in plain language really means *"I don't feel like it."*

In reality, all that matters is *simply to get started*, however commonplace that sounds. And even if we aren't "in the mood", by the time we have made a start and are concentrating on the job, we will be in the mood, just as we often don't realize we were hungry until we start eating. In most cases, we are then taken aback to conclude that it's all not nearly as difficult as we thought. By the way, this is not a modern psychological discovery; it was known to the Ancient Romans. As the philosopher Seneca aptly put it: "It is not because it is difficult that we do not dare; it is because we do not dare that things are difficult."

Or in the words of the Austrian writer Marie Ebner-Eschenbach: "It is the work that we put to one side that makes us tired, not the work that we do!" For nothing is more crippling than doing nothing.

A variation used with equal success by our little saboteurs is the *fairy tale of the right (or wrong) point in time*. Particularly in the case of important, long-overdue discussions, whether these are with your boss, your colleagues, your partner or children. It can happen that every time you are halfway to deciding to have that frank, open talk at last, the recognition suddenly dawns (bringing a sense of relief) that it is *probably the wrong time*. Our saboteur finds plenty of good reasons for this. The boss is "in a really bad mood at the moment"; your partner is much too busy right now or has other (probably more important) things on his or her plate ("I really can't burden him/her right now with relationship problems!"), and "the kids have enough stress at school anyway". So, better to wait for the right moment—perhaps we will be lucky, and it will never come! Because then we will be spared a painful row, with the resulting problems, conflicts, and consequences that may well arise.

"Please," says the saboteur, "let's not have any problems, any changes, let's just go on living in harmony, peace and happiness!" Once upon a time, so they say, there was someone who never found the right time to propose marriage to his beloved. He never understood why she finally went off with someone else. But that is probably just a fairy tale too.

Let's get this straight. Of course there are situations where it is *definitely the wrong time* for a discussion, a request or some other matter. For example, if you want to sort out your relationship with your sweetheart at the precise moment when he or she is rushing off to an important appointment. But if you never seem to find the right moment over a long period of time, then it may well be your inner saboteur pulling your strings unobserved! And be honest: are you sure that the right point in time has already come to unveil your saboteur's tricks? Be careful: there could be consequences for you ...

## Deceptive temptations

Many of us dream of temptations at some point in our lives. It seems only too human to give in to them—only warriors, heroes, and saints are said to be immune. But even for a hardened hedonist, there is little point in giving in to a temptation without fully enjoying it! If you give in only half-heartedly, only to have a bad conscience afterwards, you will hardly enjoy it properly and will be deceiving yourself. And this is exactly what happens if we willingly follow the distracting impulse that suddenly emerges. Of course it is extremely seductive just at that moment when it promises (even though only briefly) that we can exchange our negative feelings for more pleasant ones. This is where our powerful urge to avoid fear and reluctance in our lives comes into play. Pure reason is often powerless against this urge. It is as though we are drawn by an invisible power to follow the lure of diversion and be sidetracked by an easier and more pleasant activity. For the sake of immediate relief from our problems we pay the price of feeling even worse later (which, as we have seen, only increases the temptation to postpone the actual proposal yet again).

Isn't it ridiculous that we do something with a bad conscience that, only a short time after—that is, in the necessary breaks or after the work has been completed—we could enjoy with a light heart, even deservedly?

The fatal thing about the whole business is that all this happens without our noticing what is going on in our unconscious. Even worse, we secretly feel almost a *guilty pleasure* in tricking ourselves (or being tricked by our saboteur). Hans-Werner Rückert, in his book Schluss mit dem einigen Aufsanieben. Wie sie umsetzen, war sie sich vornehmen (*Stop putting it off: How to Put Your Plans Into Practice*), describes how several of his seminar participants report the *avoidance process with pleasure and enjoyment*, as though they were "*in love with something subversive* in themselves, which is opposed to their conscious aims". At the precise moment when they want to get started, they become aware of a seductive little urge: first they could dawdle a bit, watch some television, avoid the issue, and *they follow it with a smile*. [Author's italics.] The gallows humor here is easily recognized: *We may well feel a "guilty pleasure" in robbing ourselves of our time—but we ourselves are the victims!*

To be more precise, we are the victims of *deception*, not of robbery. Unlike robbery, where something is taken from the victim against his will, the *deceived* person *voluntarily* gives something away and suffers damage as a result. And that is just what we do: we deceive ourselves by pretending that avoidance is pleasant and harmless. We freely surrender part of our intention and damage ourselves in the process because our project does not get completed and, on top of this, we become less and less motivated. We? Of course it is just our "evil" saboteur who is doing this to us. We are just the "innocent" victims ... But he is already familiar with this role of scapegoat—and, as is well known, he has a thick skin!

## EXCEPTIONAL CASES

I had formed a firm resolve that in future, from 21 March (that is, at the beginning of spring), I would always ride my bicycle to the office, a distance of 5 miles. It would be much better for the environment and for my health. Also, there was a marvellous bicycle path through the park, and if it should happen to rain, there was a bus stop right in front of our house which was only two stops away from my destination. So from now on the car would stay in the garage as far as getting to work was concerned. It was wonderful—I was very happy with my new means of transport. Then, one morning—it was 7 April—it happened: I was already late, and there was a slight drizzle; the bus had just left, and I made my way to the bicycle shed. Then I saw my little saboteur heading for the garage, wagging his tail and giving me a meaningful look. His expression said it all: "If only you had got up earlier! You'll still be late for work. In this foul weather you'll not only get wet, but probably catch a massive cold. If you go by car *just this once*, it won't make the hole in the ozone layer any bigger. Anyway, you'll be able to do some shopping on the way home. And a car does need to be used once in a while." "All right—just as an exception! But tomorrow I'll go by bike again!" My little companion nodded and jumped on the back seat. Sure enough, next day I rode the bike again. But three days later I was back in the car, and then more and more often. And only yesterday I was saying to a colleague in the bar: "In this beautiful summer weather I really ought to get on my bike again some time."

### Principle No. 16
### Saboteur's rule of three:
### Let it drop—let it slide—let it be.

This little story, which may sound quite harmless, unfortunately conceals a psychological landmine. With many *changes of behavior*, which we want to retain over a lengthy period or even for ever, our inner saboteur, with a wise smile, allows us to begin the change undisturbed. He knows from experience that sooner or later we will fall into the *exception trap*. And this trap has a bad habit of destroying most of our good resolutions or at least almost unnoticeably erasing them from our lives—whether it's a new diet, becoming a non-smoker, daily jogging, drawing up a weekly schedule, keeping a regular journal or some other proposal for enriching our lives in a way intended to become a habit. The saboteur knows the enormous *attraction of old habits* and the *vulnerability and weakness of new enterprises.* Of course, the flames of enthusiasm may blaze up at the beginning, because you have at last made a start! And you tell your friends and colleagues, who congratulate and admire you (at least to your face). But secretly they may be thinking, "Your saboteur's going to get you", because they themselves have experienced this often enough. And then it comes—the *special occasion*, for which an exception can after all be made! On Grandma's birthday, of course you *must* eat a slice of her cake; you *can't possibly* drink a special toast with mineral water; walking is really *not* healthy in this miserable weather; and if someone doesn't turn up for choir practice *just once*, it's *not the end of the world*. No, none of these things is the end of the world, and your saboteur whispers confidently: "It won't matter just this once." But the first exception makes the second one much easier, and thus more likely, and quite quickly you have reached the point where "it makes no difference anyway". Before you realize it, you have let your resolution slide, and finally it will simply have been dropped without further ado. If you were to put up a memorial stone to this resolution, it would read: "After an all-too-brief life span, this young, promising resolution tragically passed away, though after only a short period of suffering in the famous exception trap!"

But no need to worry: just as an *exception*, you could allow no exceptions!

By the way, it doesn't need to be a special occasion for you to fall into the exception trap. Sometimes, for no particular outward reason, one becomes *simply careless*, and the exception creeps in unnoticed (with the second exception already in its wake). This can easily happen when we are *over-confident*. But this is just what our little saboteur has been waiting for! Can we blame him? He gazes at us with an innocent expression, grunting in a satisfied manner, while still licking his lips: "Sorry, I didn't mean to upset you! I just couldn't help myself—it was such a tempting resolution. Tasted really nice!"

## ABANDONMENT TACTICS

It seemed to have started so well, but sooner or later, with most projects, we come up against obstacles or periods of diminished motivation. These are the decisive moments in which it is important to hold on, keep going, and fight our way through. But this is associated with a certain degree of effort, which once again makes

**The little saboteurs carry a good resolution to the grave**

our little companion uncomfortable. In the very situation where, despite all the willpower we can muster, we could really do with some support, he stabs us in the back. Now we have to hold fast against his whispered words of wisdom: "This whole thing is taking up far too much of your energy!" "Is all this effort really worth it?" "After all, what are you going to get out of it?" "This isn't your strong point, you have other talents!" "Look at all the other pleasures of life that you are missing out on—you only have one life!" Then the whole thing is crowned with the challenge: "So just leave it—give up!" At this point it may often happen that we become frustrated, and begin to doubt our own capabilities and intentions. If it is really going badly, we do actually throw in the towel and declare ourselves out of the game. "Game, set and match", our saboteur says to himself, getting ready to administer consolation.

### Principle No. 17
### Better to break off cheerfully than to crawl with difficulty to one's goal.

Veterans of many a battle, on the other hand, are equal to the challenge. They simply *increase the inner pressure* and force themselves to carry on with all their might. "It would be ridiculous if I couldn't manage that! Even if I have to put my head through a brick wall!" But there is one thing they too have failed to take into account—in this case, of course, their inner saboteur. *Pressure* is something he just can't stand. And *the greater the pressure, the stronger the counter-pressure*! Now is the time for a titanic battle of inner forces to begin. The more such battles have gone in your favor in the past, the greater the probability that you will emerge the victor this time too. However, it can also happen that your little saboteur decides to mount a sit-down strike. And you have to sit this out as well. In the end, the question is whether the victory you have won by means of pressure and force isn't a Pyrrhic victory after all—but at least you didn't give up. (Other ways to hold on and stay on the ball are described in Part III, from page 97.)

## The fatal sideways glance

Martin, a law student in his final year, was facing his written examination and studying for it every day in the university library. One Wednesday morning, absolutely nothing seemed to be going right. He felt as though he couldn't understand anything any more, and decided to have a short smoking break. In the library entrance hall he met his companion in misfortune, Maggie, also with a cigarette in her hand. "By chance" their conversation turned to their "really grim" revision for the exam, they got carried away in mutual complaints about the soul-destroying swotting and cramming and came to the conclusion, almost with relief, that they "simply didn't feel like it" at the moment. So they decided to "do nothing together", and moved off in the direction of the cafeteria, where they would perhaps meet others in the same frame of mind. No, there was no chance of any more study today. Martin was not at all worried, either; after all, Maggie and two other fellow students who had joined them were not working either. Under the bistro table sat all their little saboteurs, in the best of moods. Yes, they are very sociable creatures, who like to get together with others of the same species and watch their masters and mistresses doing nothing together ...

**Principle No. 18**
**Doing nothing together is more sociable than slogging away on your own.**

Martin's break may have made perfect sense psychologically, particularly if he had already been studying continuously over a long period of time. But the insidious thing about this course of events is the *process of self-deception* which has taken place again here: since someone else in a similar situation has also given up or interrupted his intended action, it doesn't seem quite so bad to us if we also break off or make an exception. "Safety in numbers!" "Look," says an inner (and familiar) voice, "he (or she) is doing it too!" "Michael's taking a break from running." "Rita's eating a slice of cream cake too, although she's on the same diet as me!" "My colleague has put off doing his tax return as well."

You really can't fool yourself much more blatantly than with the "other people do it too" formula. Of course it can be a relief to know that we are not alone in our weaknesses (people with weaknesses are more appealing than perfectionist types). But: *It is of absolutely no use to me personally if other people are doing damage to themselves as well.*

The *sideways glance* is sometimes legitimate, but can become a fatal trap which can lead to exceptions or even to the total abandonment of our resolutions. If we need to compare ourselves with others, then we should do so with people who hold on, carry on and stay on the ball.

# 4

# WHEN THE SABOTEUR HAS WON

Well, all right, the saboteur has won, however he managed it. But our little companion doesn't simply make himself scarce with the winner's cup under his arm. He stays by our side to enjoy our defeat. He dons his nurse's cap to *comfort* us, and joins with us in a victim's lament. Unfortunately, he very rarely allows us to break down in *self-pity*, since it is in this way that he prepares the ground for future sabotage.

## THE VICTIM'S COMFORTING LAMENT

"Have you heard? Michael has started smoking again!" Barbara announced to her friends in the pub. "No! I don't believe it!" replied Robert. "Yes, it's true, and I knew he would!" said Barbara, who herself had often given up smoking, only to start up again each time after a short period of abstinence.

In fact, everyone had admired Michael when he gave up smoking on his 30th birthday. After all, he had been smoking for 15 years, and in the time leading up to his birthday it had been 20 to 30 cigarettes a day. Then suddenly, all that was over—and he had kept it up for more than three months!

No wonder the news about Michael smoking again was such a bombshell. At any rate, it immediately became the talking point of the evening. In no time the four friends, while waiting for Michael to join them, were discussing the difficulty, nay the impossibility, of shaking off a habit like smoking. Suddenly the conversation came to a halt as Michael entered the pub and approached their table. Everyone looked at him, and already suspecting what their expressions meant, he came right out with it: "Yes, it's true, I'm smoking again!" Placing a cigarette between his lips and casually lighting it, he added: "Tobacco was just stronger than I was. Anyway, it was getting unbearable—when three other people in the office are smoking, you feel like an idiot if you don't have a cigarette in your hand too." Of course, all those present understood, and Anita was quick to offer him moral support: "And the way we live is absolutely hostile to non-smokers. Wherever you go, people are puffing away. You might just as well join them." After only a short time in the circle of his friends, Michael was feeling better (how well they understood him!), and not only he, but his saboteur was feeling better too, curling up cheerfully on the floor at his feet and going to sleep.

### Principle No. 19
### Seek, and you will find a scapegoat.

Our little saboteurs are experts when it comes to *soothing a bad conscience*, lulling it with *superficial words of consolation* and *stifling feelings of guilt in the bud.* By means of sophisticated attempts at calming us, they prevent us from suddenly "waking up" and recognizing that we are permanently sabotaging ourselves (or allowing ourselves to be sabotaged?). The tactic used here is an ancient one and can be found in the Old Testament: if any one of the chosen people of God had committed a sin or some other serious offence, according to a ritual, the sin was transferred to an animal (the so-called *scapegoat*), which was then chased into the desert in his stead. This, it was assumed, would cleanse the people of the sin.

Our inner saboteurs seem to be very familiar with this tactic, and frequently practise it on us in a similar way. The *psychological mechanism* today functions as follows (see also the diagram on page 84):

If something *went wrong* or *didn't go according to plan*, we *look for the guilty party*, to whom, unconsciously or automatically, the *responsibility is transferred* for the failure which is, in fact, our own fault.

Sometimes an impersonal factor takes the blame, such as the weather, a date, the food, one's own character, one's star sign or the time. The justification goes something like this:

- "In this *weather* one simply can't …!"
- "Well, it was *Friday the 13th*!"
- "All these *business lunches*, it's impossible to lose weight!"
- "I just have a *tendency* to put on weight."
- "It's my *wife's good cooking* that makes me fat."
- "I just had *too much* to do."
- "I *can't change* the sort of person I am."
- "It's an *addiction*—I can't win."
- "I was simply *tempted*."
- "With the sort of *people I work with*, it had to go wrong."

In other cases, *anonymous forces* outside our sphere of influence are put in the pillory: circumstances, fate or even the stars. It goes like this:

- "It was *fated* not to be."
- "*It* just gets the better of me."
- "It just *wasn't meant to be*."

## The vicious circle of the victim

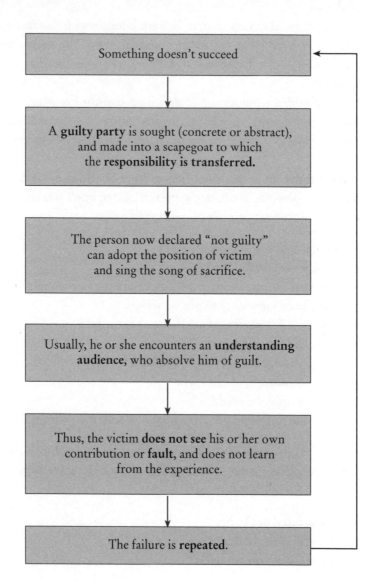

Something doesn't succeed

A **guilty party** is sought (concrete or abstract), and made into a scapegoat to which the **responsibility is transferred.**

The person now declared "not guilty" can adopt the position of victim and sing the song of sacrifice.

Usually, he or she encounters an **understanding audience,** who absolve him of guilt.

Thus, the victim **does not see** his or her own contribution or **fault,** and does not learn from the experience.

The failure is **repeated.**

- "Just *bad luck!*"
- "With this *system*, there's nothing else to be done."
- "*These days*, it's impossible to lead a healthy life."
- "The *stars* were not in our favor."
- "I'm a *Capricorn*, that's all there is to it."

Get the idea? That explains the mess you have made of things, doesn't it? (A hit list of the most common scapegoats occurring in most of the "I-just-can't-help-it" ditties is on page 86.)

By *shuffling off the responsibility*, the person in question is transformed into an apparently helpless *victim*, who can now, like Pontius Pilate in days of old, wash his hands in innocence. The reasons advanced by the victims (or their inner saboteurs) sound so convincing that the impression is created that they really had no choice but to bow to overpowering circumstances. The *victims' laments* are traditional, enticing and unfortunately almost always fall on *sympathetic ears*. It's just human nature, and "anyone who complains always has colleagues—he is never alone!" (Reinhard K. Sprenger, *Die entscheidung liegt bei Dir! Wege aus der taglichen Unzufriedenheit* [*The Decision is Yours! How to Deal with Everyday Dissatisfaction*].)

Involved in the solidarity of the "you-know-how-it-is" delusion, the others, without noticing it, become our collaborators. We expect absolution from them—and we get it. Absolution is easily granted, because those who give it naturally expect to receive it in return. This is part of the great game in which we fool ourselves and others. But the game is so widespread and has been played for so many generations that we don't notice it any more. The victims' laments are sung so often that in the end we even believe them ourselves. This process is often an *unconscious* one, and we recognize neither our own contribution that led to failure, nor the subsequent mechanism for transferring the responsibility. In this way we block the possibility of learning and really changing something in our lives. Because if other people or "the circumstances" are to blame, I don't have to change anything!

## The victim's menu of excuses

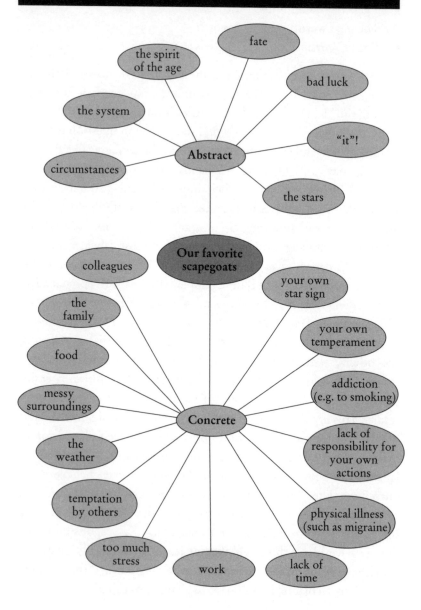

And this is precisely how we prepare the ground for the next failure. *Mistakes* that we don't recognize as such will as a rule be *repeated*. With some people, the same mistakes run through their whole lives like a red thread—without their noticing it!

The only chance of breaking out of this vicious circle (or, rather, to emerge from this fog created by our inner saboteurs) consists in *becoming aware of this automatic process*, namely that of transferring *responsibility*, and in an honest and matter-of-fact manner seeking the causes of failure within ourselves. In this way we once again assume responsibility, are able to learn from experience and next time perhaps change something in our lives. Or, to put it another way: *Unconscious models determine our lives—until we finally see through them. Because only when we know what we are doing can we begin to do things differently.*

Please don't take this to mean that the recognition of a mistake automatically leads to its not being repeated. We will commit it even more often if it is an old model in the system of our habits. But each time there is an increasing chance that you will do things differently! This is expressed particularly well in the following text by Sogyal Rinpoche. The prerequisite is the readiness to wake up, give up the smokescreen games and consciously take over responsibility again!

*Autobiography in five chapters*

1. *I walk down the street.*
   *There is a deep hole in the pavement.*
   *I fall in.*
   *I am lost … I am helpless.*
   *It isn't my fault.*
   *It takes an endless time to get out again.*

2. *I walk down the same street.*
   *There is a deep hole in the pavement.*

*I pretend not to see it.*
*I fall in again.*
*I can't believe I am in the same place again.*
*But it isn't my fault.*
*It still takes a long time to get out.*

3. *I walk down the same street.*
   *There is a deep hole in the pavement.*
   *I see it.*
   *I fall in again—out of habit.*
   *My eyes are open.*
   *I know where I am.*
   *It's my own fault.*
   *I get out immediately.*

4. *I walk down the same street.*
   *There is a deep hole in the pavement.*
   *I walk around it.*

5. *I walk down a different street.*

From: *The Tibetan Book of Living and Dying*, Sogyal Rinpoche, Patrick D. Gaffney, Andrew Harvey.

## DESTRUCTIVE LAMENTS OF THE LOSER

Now the time has come when you must take care not to score an own goal. Taking over responsibility doesn't mean beating yourself up and condemning yourself as a loser. Some people tend to dissolve into self-pity after only the slightest setback, and declaim in uncompromising fashion: "There you are, you see, I can't do *anything* right!" "What's the point of *anything*? Whatever I do goes wrong!" "I just can't do it, I'll never get *anything* done properly!"

This is the quickest way to setting yourself up for further failures or, before long, giving up any new projects at all.

### Principle No. 20
### Always—everything—never: the typical loser's mixture!

If your inner saboteur actually sings you this sort of loser's lament, just shout at him: "Shut up! What nonsense!" Yes, that kind of self-disparagement is nonsense (even if it's a question of a frequently occurring model of *inner self-dismantling*).

In order to become conscious as quickly as possible of the falseness of such thought processes, please have a pen and paper to hand *right now*. The following little exercise won't take more than five or ten minutes. Make a note of all your successes over the last 12 months, whether professional or private. And please, no qualifications along the lines of: "Well, anyone can do that!" or "That doesn't really count, because …" We are now considering success, positive things, good results, not their relative value—because that again would be another self-sabotage mechanism.

However many successes are on your list after five minutes, you have certainly quite clearly contradicted the notion that you can do *nothing* right or that *everything* goes wrong for you! And if your little saboteur still won't leave you in peace with his insistence that you are a loser, simply chase him out of the door for a while. (The best way of dealing with him when he gets back in through the back door will be explained in Part III of this book.)

| Tricks and tactics of the little saboteur at a glance | |
| --- | --- |
| **I. He prevents the taking of a decision in advance by means of:** | |
| 1. Impossibility tactics | "It can't be done." "No one could be expected to do that." "It just won't work!" |

| Tricks and tactics of the little saboteur at a glance (continued) | |
|---|---|
| **I. He prevents the taking of a decision in advance by means of:** | |
| 2. The game of the magic hat | Fulfilment of duty<br>False consideration for others<br>The cloak of morality |
| 3. Non-commitment | The words "must", "should", "could"<br>The word "one" |
| 4. Delaying tactics | "I can't do it yet."<br>"First I need to …" |
| 5. Playing it down | "It's not as bad as all that."<br>"Nothing to worry about."<br>"Other people do it too/don't do it either." |
| 6. Not my responsibility | "Why me?"<br>"It's not my responsibility."<br>"Other people could do it better." |
| 7. Traditional clichés | "We've always done it that way!"<br>"We've never done it that way!" |
| 8. Playing it safe | "Don't take the risk."<br>"A bird in the hand …" |
| 9. The easy life | "Just sit down and relax." |
| **II. He waters down the decision by means of:** | |
| 1. Just wanting to try | "I'll try to …"<br>"I'll just see if I can manage it …" |
| 2. Smoke-screen tactics | Vague formulations<br>Comparatives such as "more", "more often", "healthier", etc.<br>The words "some time", "soon", "some time or other" |
| 3. The free spirit | No plan, no deadline |
| 4. Herculean plans | Taking on too much ("Now I'm going to get right down to it!") |

| Tricks and tactics of the little saboteur at a glance (continued) | |
| --- | --- |
| **III. He sabotages the realization of our plans by means of:** | |
| 1. Diversionary tactics | Not in the mood yet<br>Just quickly doing x<br>Must tidy up first<br>Allowing oneself a treat<br>Spontaneous actions |
| 2. Exceptional cases | The "special" occasion<br>"Just this once won't hurt" |
| 3. Abandonment tactics | "Much too much effort!"<br>"It's not worth it!"<br>"You only have one life." |
| 4. The fatal sideways glance | "He/she is doing it too isn't/doing it either."<br>Doing nothing together/"sinning" together |
| **IV. And afterwards he makes us:** | |
| 1. Play the victim | Find scapegoats<br>"I just can't help it!"<br>Seeking absolution |
| 2. Play the self-destructive loser | "I can't do anything right!"<br>" What's the point of anything?" |

The checklist on the double-page spread that follows gives you the opportunity to become aware of the *most common* statements and tactics that are used again and again to trick you by your inner saboteur.

It's very helpful, after filling in this table, to note the most important tactics once again on a separate sheet of paper (your Top Ten, as it were, that is, the tricks that you most often fall for, in your opinion). When you have become properly aware of these tactics, you will probably in future notice much more easily and frequently the occasions when you are fooling yourself. Or in other words:

## Your little saboteur's favorite sayings and tactics

For each saying or tactic, enter points from 1 ("I'd never say that") to 6 ("I know that one only too well"). Then mark your saboteur's most frequent tricks, and make a note of them separately.

| Saying/tactic | Saboteur activity | | | | | |
|---|---|---|---|---|---|---|
| | *Mild level* | | | *High level* | | |
| **I. Before the decision** | 1 | 2 | 3 | 4 | 5 | 6 |
| "I can't do it!" | | | | | | |
| "I can't manage that!" | | | | | | |
| "That won't work." | | | | | | |
| "No one could be expected to do that." | | | | | | |
| "It's much too difficult." | | | | | | |
| "It's not worth it." | | | | | | |
| "Anyway, what's the point?" | | | | | | |
| Supposed sense of duty | | | | | | |
| False consideration for others | | | | | | |
| "It's just not done!" (morality) | | | | | | |
| "I must, should, could …" | | | | | | |
| "Actually, I shouldn't … so much." | | | | | | |
| "One should, one ought to …" | | | | | | |
| "I can't do it yet, first I would have to …" | | | | | | |
| "It doesn't matter." | | | | | | |
| "It's not a big deal." | | | | | | |
| "Other people do it (don't do it)." | | | | | | |
| "That's not our job." | | | | | | |
| "I'm not responsible for that." | | | | | | |
| "What has this got to do with me?" | | | | | | |
| "Other people could do it better." | | | | | | |
| "It's always been like that." | | | | | | |
| "I've never done it (like that)." | | | | | | |
| "Where would we be if …?" | | | | | | |
| "Better not take the risk." | | | | | | |
| "Suppose it goes wrong?" | | | | | | |
| "A bird in the hand …" | | | | | | |
| "Relax, take it easy." | | | | | | |
| **II. The decision** | 1 | 2 | 3 | 4 | 5 | 6 |
| "I will try/want to try …" | | | | | | |
| "I want to live a healthier life." | | | | | | |

| Your little saboteur's favorite sayings and tactics (continued) | | | | | | |
|---|---|---|---|---|---|---|
| Saying/tactic | Saboteur activity | | | | | |
| | Mild level | | | High level | | |
| | 1 | 2 | 3 | 4 | 5 | 6 |
| "… work less." | | | | | | |
| "… do more sport." | | | | | | |
| "… live more economically." | | | | | | |
| "… earn more money." | | | | | | |
| "… some time soon …" | | | | | | |
| "Some time I will have to …" | | | | | | |
| No plans | | | | | | |
| No deadlines | | | | | | |
| "Now I'm really going to get to grips with it!" | | | | | | |
| "Now I'm going to sort things out properly!" | | | | | | |
| "Now I'll really show them!" | | | | | | |
| Taking on too much | | | | | | |
| **III. Sabotage of decision implementation** | 1 | 2 | 3 | 4 | 5 | 6 |
| "I'm simply not in the mood (yet)." | | | | | | |
| Need to tidy up a bit first. | | | | | | |
| "I'll just quickly …" | | | | | | |
| Have a bit of a rest first | | | | | | |
| Make a quick phone call/check the post/do some shopping | | | | | | |
| "Plenty of time for that!" | | | | | | |
| Or other distraction | | | | | | |
| "Just this once!" | | | | | | |
| "Just today, as an exception." | | | | | | |
| "As it's a special occasion …" | | | | | | |
| "That would take too much energy." | | | | | | |
| "It's not worth the effort." | | | | | | |
| "You only have one life!" | | | | | | |
| "Just leave it!" | | | | | | |
| "He/she's taking a break too!" | | | | | | |
| "He/she hasn't done it yet either!" | | | | | | |
| "It's not my fault …" | | | | | | |
| "I can't help it …" | | | | | | |
| "I'm not achieving anything, anyway." | | | | | | |
| "Anyway, what's the point of it all?" | | | | | | |

when your little saboteur is once again ready to push you into that hole in the pavement that Sogyal Rinpoche was talking about. The sooner you notice your little enemy's schemes, the better is your chance of switching over and changing your behavior—that is, "walking down a different street".

A personal "hit list" of tricks and tactics can provide valuable help. Some participants in my seminars found it helped them to have their "Top Ten" list ready to hand, so that whenever their personal saboteurs made attempts to foil their plans, they immediately thought: "Well, which saying or trick are we going to try today?" And once caught in the act, the saboteur would often make a speedy exit. Some of these participants would keep their hit list in their trouser pocket for a while, others had written them out on a page in their diaries, and the technology freaks, as one would expect, had entered them in their personal organizers. A friend of mine had even put together a poster for his "smallest room", which included his Top Ten and an image of a mischievously grinning saboteur. As you see, there are no limits to the imagination on the path to self-awareness. And it might even amuse your little companion, for these saboteurs are not lacking in a sense of humor!

At this point, a little pause might be called for. Before you turn to Part III of this book, it would be helpful if you would take another five minutes to clarify your *personal goals* in the near future for your dealings with your personal saboteur. In which areas of your life do you need to confront him, tame him or just get wise to his tricks? Which of his tricks and tactics do you want to avoid falling for in future? The following table shows how this sort of plan might look:

**I want to sort things out with my inner saboteur
so that within ...**

the next two months:

**❶** _____

**❷** _____

**❸** _____

the next twelve months:

**❶** _____

**❷** _____

**❸** _____

Now it is time to get a little closer to your personal enemy, to get to know him better and better, and to find out how you can deal with him more confidently and get a few things straight with him. In Part III, which follows now, you will find help for this, and tips not only for taming your little saboteur, but even for transforming him from your worst enemy into your best friend.

# PART III

# STRATEGIES FOR DEALING WITH THE LITTLE SABOTEUR

Now we're coming to the point—namely the question of the most sensible way of coming to terms with this peculiar companion who gives you so much trouble.

For a start, it's important to recognize and accept certain *natural laws* pertaining to "coexistence" with the little saboteur, at least if you want to spare yourself much unnecessary effort and energy-consuming detours. Here are the four basic rules for dealing with him:

**1. We can't run away from the little saboteur ...** This species is extremely affectionate and always devoted and loyal to its current master or mistress. The saboteur is always following at your heels and refuses to be shaken off. However fast you run, even if you fly to the remotest regions of the planet, your inner saboteur will become a stowaway and accompany you. Many a traveller has thought he could manage to shake his inner companion off and believed himself to be entirely alone on his journey. But as soon as he found he didn't have the confidence to pay a compliment to the pretty air hostess, he noticed that his little saboteur was on board!

**... and we can't drive him away!** The little saboteur always comes back. Even if they are rudely chased out of the house, after a short time, there they are, back again, even if they have to use the back door. Your little saboteur will be grinning at you with a mischievous smile through the crack of the door, while you are perhaps already celebrating the fact that you are now in sole charge of your life. Big mistake! And please don't even think about trying some kind of security measures. A saboteur knows all the tricks for creeping in again. What's more, he is a master of disguise and of making himself invisible—he can have been back at your side for quite a while before you notice him.

**2. We can't keep the little saboteur permanently locked up.** Many people try to confine their inner saboteur in the deepest dungeons of their personality, by putting their lives under the "firm grip of iron discipline". But your little enemy will not be conquered in this way—on the contrary: he has only been banished to the "realm of shadows of your personality", and there, invisible and thus even more dangerous, like all prisoners he will devote all his energy to escaping and even, in some cases, taking his revenge—all according to how merciless and harsh his incarceration was for him. And he knows one thing: severe discipline can't be endured for a long time. So anyone who locks up his inner saboteur will, time and again, be forced to let him out again.

**3. We must not allow the little saboteur to take over.** In a state which gives way to all resistance, the result is anarchy. If we have no will of our own and follow the saboteur blindly, sooner or later we will not get anything done, and all our plans will go to the dogs. So this is definitely not the solution, as simple as it may seem. You must therefore give as good as you get—I will tell you how in a moment.

**4. We must learn to live with our little saboteur—to tame him.** To start with, this means accepting your inner saboteur as your life companion—even a necessary one; developing the wish to come to terms intensively and honestly with him, in order to realize clearly on which occasion he interferes with our plans, and what tricks he uses to do so. At the same time, it is of course a case of finding strategies and means which enable us, in spite of our little companion—even hand-in-hand with him—to realize our aims and intentions. In this way, he can even become no longer our worst enemy, but our best friend.

Even when you go on holiday, your little saboteur always
comes along

# 5
## ACCEPTING THE LITTLE SABOTEUR

Hector Steel was a real fighter, hard as nails and very disciplined. He seemed to have his life well under control. From childhood, his father had taught him to struggle against the "greatest enemy" in a person's life, the inner saboteur, and to win repeated victories over him. Like his father, Hector was merciless with himself and others, and entirely ruthless when it came to weakness, leniency or "sissy" behavior. He had made great progress in his career by means of extreme toughness and the lack of scruples that he considered indispensable, but he never had time to enjoy his successes, for he was always pushing on to the next goal and was thus constantly under pressure. He ignored repeated attacks of flu and recurrent stomach ache, saying "It's all in the mind", just as he did his chronic breathlessness and the ever-more-frequent stabbing pains in his chest. No giving in! No illness, no saboteur would get him down!

Three days after his 42nd birthday he fell dead in his office from a stroke. His little saboteur was buried with him. The latter's diary was later published in the local *Saboteurs' Gazette*. It showed that Hector's saboteur really did not have an easy time with him. He had tried all his tricks to get his master to show a little more humanity towards himself and others, to laze about once in a while, simply to enjoy life and allow himself some weaknesses. But in vain! The saboteur actually liked Hector and was attached to him, but he had no chance against Hector's toughness. In the end he became resigned to the superior powers of his master and arranged that at least his notes should be published after his death. Perhaps they could help the saboteur assigned to Hector's five-year-old son Simon to see to it that at least he would go about his life in a less self-punishing manner.

Hector's attitude is unfortunately a common one. Many people, particularly men, see the inner saboteur only as an enemy to be outsmarted, vanquished or even killed. Martial expressions such as "battle", "victory or defeat", "kill and destroy", "toughness and severity", "overcoming and subjugating", are characteristic of their vocabulary when they think about their little saboteur. Not really surprising when you take into account the fact that the concept of the inner saboteur was used above all in a German military context. For example, Meint Harms wrote in a monograph published in 1954 about the inner saboteur:

"When a soldier was getting ready for the attack, and for fear of his life stayed under cover, or if he was tempted to give up in some other way, or if he had made a mistake and felt tempted … to cover up his mistake, that is, when his natural anxiety was provoking him not to do something he should be doing, or to do something he should not be doing, this fear, in the graphic language of the German *Wehrmacht*, was called 'the inner *Schweinehund*' (the inner saboteur). A substantial part of military training was directed at teaching how to overcome the 'inner *Schweinehund*'—with remarkable success!"

Remarkable perhaps, but hardly praiseworthy when we consider that this attitude contributed to Europe being reduced to rubble and the loss of millions of lives.

This battle mentality arises ultimately from a *black-and-white* way of thinking that separates not only the outside world into "good and evil", but also the inner world of one's own personality. According to this pattern, only discipline, toughness, achievement and overcoming obstacles are perceived as good, and giving in, dawdling, lazing around, and general weakness as bad. Of course, this is a way of combating the inner saboteur and need not always lead to such extreme phenomena as in the story of Hector Steel. But in any case it is a very strenuous method and also, even if most people are not aware of this, a *battle against ourselves*, at least against a part of ourselves. And the experience and awareness attained by most people is, paradoxically, as follows:

**The more you battle against your inner saboteur,
the more often you will have to deal with him.**

Or, as a seminar participant recently expressed it very aptly:

**The greater the pressure,
the more aggressive the saboteur.**

So the more we put ourselves under pressure, the less we allow ourselves to relax and enjoy life, the more viciously the inner saboteur will react.

In my own country, Germany, to a degree hardly found anywhere else in the world, we tend to put ourselves constantly under pressure. Is this why so much effort is expended in German-speaking countries in the battle against the inner *Schweinehund* or saboteur? In English-speaking countries, the "pig-dog" or similar creature is as unknown as it is in France, Greece, Italy or Spain, for example. Not for nothing is there more of the equanimity and *savoir vivre* to be found in those countries that are often lacking in our perfectionist, performance-oriented society.

So far, we have come to recognize one thing: the little saboteur does not allow himself to be outwitted forever (unless, like Hector, we take him with us to the grave). Because in cases of conflict he sets up his battle headquarters in the stomach, and forms an alliance with our feelings; for most people he is the permanent driving force. But there is also a very different way for us to deal with this apparently congenital companion.

According to the overwhelming opinion of today's psychologists, it is not a question of battling against, suppressing, condemning or even destroying something in ourselves, but rather of being aware and *integrating* certain aspects of ourselves. For:

**As long as we are battling with part of ourselves, we are battling against ourselves. Only when we are able to accept and integrate this part of ourselves will we make any progress.**

Whether we like it or not, the inner saboteur is *part of our personality structure*, and we have no choice but to recognize and accept this fact, just as with some other aspect of ourselves that we perhaps may not like and which makes us suffer. *Growth and development of the personality* are basically only possible by means of *self-acceptance*— not by doing battle with part of your personality. "Acceptance", however, does not mean that I totally identify with this partial aspect of myself, or reduce myself to this aspect! In other words:

**I do have an inner saboteur, but I am not identical to him.**

Let's assume that our personality consists of various parts, which we name according to their various functions. Thus, for example, we find in ourselves, on the one hand a planner, a disciplinarian, a fighter, but also a *bon viveur*, a sensualist, a creative artist, a sad person, a happy one, and many others. And beside all these and possibly other facets of our personality, we now and then encounter a part which gives us trouble and seems to sabotage our plans: our inner saboteur.

The longer and the more intensively we tackle this extremely curious aspect of our personality, the more inevitable becomes the realization that in fact it is a *necessary* part of our personality structure—one that is fulfilling a very *meaningful* function in our lives. Our little saboteur after all only "turns nasty" when we do not appreciate him and allow him no latitude—or if we put him (and thus ourselves) under too much pressure.

But what does his "true character" look like? Many character studies of saboteurs allow us to recognize the following, highly interesting profile with various, partly contradictory (ambivalent) aspects:

- Our first impression is that our little enemy *sabotages our plans*, plays tricks on us, prevents us from achieving our aims and operates as an annoying opponent and hindrance in our lives.

- However, in many cases our saboteur only wants to *preserve us from asking too much of ourselves, overwork and overexertion*, and stop us exceeding our own limits in a self-damaging way because of the senseless excesses of today's achievement-oriented mentality.

- Basically, *our companion wants only what is best for us*. In particular, he wants to make sure that things go well for us immediately, right at this very moment and as quickly as possible (again); he therefore strives to satisfy our basic needs in the simplest and most obvious way. He lives in the here and now, with *no concept of the phenomenon called the "future"*. Neither is he *open to abstract ideas and plans*.

There are little saboteurs all over the world

- In other respects, our inner saboteur is *like a little child*. He likes an easy life, likes to play, do silly things, be somewhat chaotic at times, eat sweet things, snuggle up, take a nap, laze around and all sorts of other things that children like doing. Like a child, he is mischievous, playful, tries to play tricks on us, is sometimes unruly and rarely obedient. But his prime concern is not to harm us; he just wants to have fun and spread wellbeing in the present, and thus opposes everything which seems to work against this aim.

This character profile shows us entirely *new aspects* of handling our inner saboteur, but only if we encounter him when we are in a state of alertness and awareness.

1. We can *pay attention to him* when he tries to direct us to *meaningful limits* in our lives (in particular when we are once again on the point of overdoing things). Like Tom DeMarco in his book *Slack: Getting Past Burnout, Busywork, and the Myth of Total Efficiency*, our inner saboteur in many cases also demands a meaningful "right to be slack". This, of course, means *paying attention to ourselves*.

2. We can *learn from him* to *be a child again* from time to time. In other words, to live in the present, to ensure our temporary wellbeing, to enjoy ourselves, to wind down, take things easy, enjoy, wallow, release our inner rascal and prankster, to be spontaneous, do something really crazy, to cry or laugh, and discover our childish potential anew. So many things that would have been a hindrance to the soldiers at the front are those that we now urgently need again in our everyday lives!

3. *Nevertheless*, we need to *set boundaries* for our inner saboteurs, in order to realize our meaningful goals without allowing ourselves to be sabotaged by him in the process. As with a small child, we can't allow him unlimited freedom. He too needs to

learn that it's always a question of pulling oneself together again, overcoming weakness and seeing things through on the way to one's goal.

Allow your saboteur a certain niche where he is able to live. Take him by the hand, talk to him and, in return, learn how to listen to him too. If necessary, negotiate with him—but stop constantly doing battle with him! The more you accept *him*, the less he will oppose *your* intentions. And if you are still convinced that an inner battle is essential, at least look on it as a playful competition. And one more tip:

**Let your little saboteur win from time to time,
and then he will let you win too.**

In this way you can *turn a presumed enemy into an ally*. In time, you will recognize ever more quickly when you need to listen to your saboteur as to a good adviser (almost as an envoy from your "wise inner voice"), and when it's better to set boundaries and overcome his resistance. Try to preserve *a good balance between meaningful "saboteur times" and times for action*!

Some time, ask your saboteur *what purpose* he is pursuing *for you* in your life, what he is trying to achieve for you! Our little companion always has a positive intention (even if he seems to be hindering us); he is acting in our interests. What his exact intention is, however, will vary from person to person and also often from situation to situation. The closer you get to him, the sooner you will find out and the easier it will be for you to accept your inner opponent!

I recommend that you stop reading now, take a pen and paper and answer the following four questions:

1. How would *your* life look if you had *no* inner saboteur? What would be the positive and negative results of this for you?

2. If your inner saboteur—whom you have perhaps encountered so far only as an opponent—were to pursue a *positive purpose* in your life, what would it be? (Of course it could be several purposes!)
3. In which areas of your life do you tend again and again to take on too much, to demand too much of yourself?
4. What could you perhaps relearn from your inner saboteur?

The realizations you have made by now will help you to see the phenomenon of the inner saboteur in a different light and also to accept your own saboteur more easily. Develop a closer relationship with him, tame him, and then he will sabotage you less often. Rather, he may even accompany you, wagging his tail, when you go for a run, or help you with the tidying up! Allow yourself to be surprised!

Hector Steel's son Simon, unlike his father, is said to have learned to devote himself to his saboteur. Apparently he succeeded in making his original enemy into an ally. His saboteur actually leaves him alone when he is working, because he knows that Simon does allow himself enough time for breaks and leisure. If ever he finds himself on the point of overdoing things, his ally only needs to tap him on the shoulder and utter a little grunt, and Simon knows that he has to change down a gear. If he undertakes some new project, for example, getting up earlier in the morning, then there may be a tug-of-war, but they both enjoy it. And if Simon has plans that his little companion would prefer to avoid, Simon takes his hand and they move forward together. At least, that's what was reported in the latest issue of the *Saboteurs' Gazette*!

Is something like this really possible? Only you can decide. The sections that follow will tell you how to approach your projects without fear of sabotage.

# 6

# THE POWER OF LANGUAGE

*Being honest with ourselves* and having *an optimistic view* form the foundation of *independent, responsible action* and *successful achievement of goals*. It will help us, for one thing, if we learn to translate certain phrases from the little saboteur's language into their *real* meaning; in other words, to *decode* them. This will destroy the illusion that we use repeatedly to deceive ourselves. For another, we can use *positive rewording* (changing the label, so to speak) to achieve a new solution and success-oriented view, motivating us more strongly to act.

## CORRECT TRANSLATION LEADS TO HONESTY

Our inner saboteur will keep on trying to trick us with its *special wording* (as you have read in Part II), preventing us from taking a clear and definite decision, or later on blurring our view of our own responsibility. Its greatest successes are due to the *language of impossibility*. It may of course be that a particular decision doesn't make sense for us and therefore we shouldn't take it in the first place. However, we will only *consciously* be aware of this if we are *able to translate* the little saboteur's code *immediately*, in that

111

particular situation—and if we are honest with ourselves. As a reminder, here is a little aid to translation:

| What the little saboteur really means | |
|---|---|
| Phrase | Translation |
| " I can't"<br>"I'll never make it"<br>"That's impossible"<br>"No one could do that"<br>"That's far too hard"<br>"Impossible"<br>"It's not worth it"<br>"It's completely pointless"<br>etc. | "I don't want to"<br>or<br>"I don't trust myself to" |
| "I haven't got the time" | "I'd rather do something else" |
| "I'm not motivated" | "I don't feel like it" |
| "I did try!" | "I didn't really want to"<br>or<br>"It wasn't important enough to me" |

The quicker you decode these statements, and the more honest you are with yourself, the easier it will be to get your inner slacker to give up on these tactics. Just like a small child, it will see that a particular line of approach is no longer working. The little saboteur might try a few more times ("Well, you never know …"), but then it will say to itself, "It's impossible! It's not worth it, none of us can manage that!" And off it will go (sulking a little at first) to its box of tricks, to find some new tactics.

Apart from the language of impossibility, it's vital to translate the widely-used "one", "you", "someone" and similar phrases. Most people (or their inner saboteurs) like to hide behind expressions such as "one" or the vague use of "you" when they either mean "I" (for example, "You can't just …" instead of "I don't trust myself to …", or if they don't want to do something themselves (for instance, the sentence "Someone ought to tidy this place up" really means "Somebody ought to do it, but not me, thank you very much"). *One could add all sorts of things to this list, but I don't have the time!*

## CHANGE THE LABEL — GET A NEW POINT OF VIEW

The *quality* of the words we use to "label" our plans is very important for the level of motivation we have to act.

### *A "World-View of Opportunity"*

An elderly lady I telephoned recently said at the end of the conversation that she *had to* go into her garden now, she hadn't yet got round to it today. In answer to my astonished question as to why she *had to*, she replied, "Well, I *have to* enjoy it from time to time, as I've got such a lovely garden!" Now I have known this lady for a very long time, and we usually discuss most things quite openly. So I asked her if she had ever noticed that she used the words *"I have to"* for almost everything she planned to do. According to her language, she *had to* eat breakfast, then she *had to* go shopping, she *had to* prepare lunch, then she *had to* clear up the kitchen, she *had to* take a siesta and later she *had to* go to tea at her neighbor's ... Indeed, she even *had to* go to a concert now and then, she *had to* accept dinner invitations and several times a year she *had to* go away on holiday. No, she hadn't ever noticed this, but she couldn't quite understand what was so odd about this use of language; after all, it was simply how things were: "You *have to* ..."

There are in fact many activities and actions which are necessary and which we very sensibly perform in order to live in a civilized manner, achieve our goals, and do good for ourselves and for others. The question is whether it's sensible to refer to and experience all things as something we *have to* do, or whether it might not be better to describe them using "can", "may" or "want to". The result may not be any different, but *psychologically* the difference should not be underestimated. The *wording* of our plans is much more important than most people realize. For our words not only reflect how we perceive and experience the world, but our language also affects our feelings. Or, to put it slightly differently:

**Our choice of words not only influences our thoughts and our view of things, but also our feelings.**

Language, as the philosopher Martin Heidegger said, is the house of being.

People who constantly refer to their plans (to themselves or to others) as something they have to do experience their actions more as a duty, as fulfilling the expectations of others. Their lives seem to offer them few opportunities for choice. The same applies to the widely-used "*should* and *ought*" expressions; one should or ought to do something. Instead, say that you *want to* or *would like to* do something, because you have decided to do it. This apparently tiny *change of label* psychologically opens a new world of choice and of your own priorities. This is the *world-view of opportunity* instead of pressure!

**If you say "I have to" instead of "I want to", you will change inner pressure into an *inner demand to do something*.**

Your inner saboteur will be much less noticeable if you say to yourself, "Now I want to fill in my tax return", "I feel like clearing out the basement now", "I want to and I will give up smoking!"

than if you feel that you *have to* do all these things. As early as 1779, the German philosopher and poet Gottfried Ephraim Lessing had his character Nathan the Wise say in the play of the same name, "*No one has to have to!*" This Nathan really was wise. That has to—oops, excuse me!—that *could* give us something to think about, don't you agree?

> **So change your labels, and in future, instead of "I have to", "I ought to" or "I should", say "I want to", "I'd like to", "I can", "I will" or "I have the opportunity to".**

Yes, you did read it right: "I have the opportunity to"! This enables you to go a step further. There is an excellent exercise that helps you achieve an interesting and motivation-boosting *change of perspective*: just replace "have to" with "have the opportunity to". You might be a bit skeptical at the start (and your inner saboteur won't know what to make of it). But just make a start with all the things that you think you have to do from morning till night: "I *have the opportunity* to get up early, I *have the opportunity to* take a shower, I *have the opportunity to* eat breakfast, *the opportunity to* take my children to school, *the opportunity to* go to work …"

"Excuse me, that's going too far!" you, or at any rate your inner slacker, will now cry. "*The opportunity to work*, that's a bit of an exaggeration! I *have to* go to work, never mind having the *opportunity*!" Really? Well, just imagine you didn't have any work, you *had no opportunity* to work! Millions of people everywhere have *no opportunity* to work at present, because they can't find a job (of course, some don't want to, either). Imagine what your life would be like without work (never mind the financial difficulties). For most people, a life of idleness, even if they had enough money, would be lacking in fulfillment and rather empty. If you agree with the above, how does "I *have the opportunity* to work" sound now?

One could of course point out that work has not only positive but also many negative aspects: stress, rivalry, difficulties, problems … but imagine if there were no problems to solve in your work— meaning no challenges for you. How long could you stand such a job? Or, to phrase the question differently, how much fun would you have if you were a tennis player playing long-term against a partner whom you wiped off the court 6–0, 6–0, 6–0 every time? Most successful people are of the opinion that a life without difficulties or challenges would be extremely dull, and even those who have made it to the top are almost always looking for new challenges—or else they sink into lethargy and boredom. (We will discuss the differing effects of challenges in our lives in more detail from page 126 onwards.)

Now back to our little exercise. Make a note of all things that, in your opinion, you *have to* do in your life and for each of the tasks you have written down imagine how your life would be if you were *unable* to do this because you had no opportunity. Brief reflection here can lead to a double effect: not only does it give a relative view of the weight of duty involved with "must/have to", but often also makes you grateful for the many opportunities there are in your life. And don't forget: you even *have the opportunity* to learn how to tame your little saboteur …

Although the elderly lady I mentioned at the beginning of this chapter had in the past asked me to keep my well-meant advice and words of wisdom for my books, seminars and lectures, rather than attempting to teach her at her age, she did listen to my comments very carefully this time (apparently not without some success), and in the end she remarked, "Well then, much as I value our friendship, I'd like to end this discussion now and *have the opportunity* to go into the garden, as I *want* to enjoy it at least for a short while today!" Ouch, I thought suddenly, I'll *have to* be a bit more diplomatic in future. As I made this resolution, my inner saboteur, with a wicked smile, ate it …

## *Focus on solutions*

Asking the right questions can help find a way out of a situation we have labeled as insoluble. The tables below will show you some possibilities.

If you focus on *solutions*, your chances of finding them are considerably better. Your *perspective* changes. The little saboteurs have learned that by now.

| Solutions for apparently insoluble problems | |
| --- | --- |
| Instead of saying: | Ask yourself: |
| "I can't do that" | "What's the best way of doing this?" |
| "That won't work" | "What alternative solutions are there?" |
| "I'm stuck" | "How can I continue?" |
| "I'll never make it" | "What would be the first step?" |

*Recently a little saboteur in the saboteurs' school put up its hand and said, "I'm stuck. My owner can see through all my strategies. I don't know what to do!" Calm and smiling, the saboteur instructor replied, "Well, how can you continue? What possible solutions are there? What would be the next step?" With a single bound the little gremlin had disappeared into its box of tricks to develop its creativity ...*

| Rewording the negative as positive | |
| --- | --- |
| In future, view | as |
| Problems | Tasks and opportunities |
| Difficulties | Challenges and opportunities for training |
| Mistakes | Orientation aids and learning opportunities |
| Failures | Incidents on the path to success |

It's best to give problems and difficulties new labels right at the start, making them into preliminary stages for subsequent success. This isn't putting on rose-tinted spectacles. It will have a positive influence on your point of view and your method of action.

Presumably, your inner slacker will have no objections to this "relabeling" and may then not be quite so tempted to sabotage you! It will however be even less tempted if you apply the right methods from *motivational psychology*.

# 7

# THE NOBLE ART OF SELF-MOTIVATION

Sixty children, all about four years old, sat in one large room, each child looking at a delicious marshmallow on the table in front of him or her. Their mouths were starting to water when they heard the nursery supervisor say loud and clear, "If you want, you can eat the marshmallow now—but if you can manage to wait a quarter of an hour, you will get another two marshmallows!" They were shown on the big clock that hung on the wall where all could see it when the quarter hour would have passed.

What followed in the next 15 minutes was utterly fascinating. About a third of the children didn't hesitate for long and devoured their treats with obvious enjoyment ("A bird in the hand is better than two in the bush"). However, that was the end of the fun as far as they were concerned. Another third did in fact try to wait for the time specified in order to obtain the promised reward (more or less in the hope of jam tomorrow), but after a few minutes they were overwhelmed by the attraction of the marshmallow in front of them, with one child after another weakening, grabbing and then eating the sweet object—even though with somewhat mixed feelings. The final third of the children, in contrast, remained steadfast. Some looked away, others covered their eyes or held their noses or tried to find some way to take their minds off the marshmallow. At any rate, they made it—and, beaming with delight, they received the two further marshmallows they had been promised.

That was the first part of the so-called Marshmallow Test described by the Harvard psychologist Daniel Goleman in his bestseller, *Emotional Intelligence*. But the really interesting results only came out in the second half of the test. The further development of the 60 children was monitored for 30 years, and of particular interest was the question of the test subjects' future success in life. And indeed it became clear that those who at an early stage had the *ability* to *abstain from short-term satisfaction in favor of long-term gain* were by far the more successful in later life.

Success, as Goleman's main proposition claims (a claim also made by many other motivational psychologists) is not primarily a matter of analytical-academic intelligence (the sort that is generally measured in IQ tests) but mainly of so-called *emotional intelligence*, that is the capacity to handle one's own emotions and those of other people in the best possible way. The main factors here are the capacities for *self-motivation* and *self-control*.

Just like the four-year-olds in the Marshmallow Experiment, we adults are also constantly concerned with this question: How can we rein in our own little inner saboteur, who has no sense of time and wants to satisfy all needs straight away, in order to gain our long-term goals and the greater rewards associated with them?

## "K.I.T.A." AND "CARROT"

*How can you get a stubborn donkey to move?* This question was put by the American motivation researcher, Herzberg. The "Herzberg Model" named after him is to be found in Vera F. Birkenbihl's *Erfolgstraining: Schaffen Sie Ihre Wirklichkeit Selbst*

[Training for Success: Create Your Own Reality]. The model shows two motivational strategies that are used to move not only stubborn donkeys, but by most people to motivate themselves and others.

## Strategy 1: K.I.T.A.

The letters—please excuse my language—stand for "kick in the ass". You administer this to the donkey and, if it is done firmly enough, the donkey will move. This, therefore, is the well-tried motivational method using *pressure, threats, punishment, sanctions, shouting, reproaches, playing on a sense of guilt,* and so on. This method does work! Its use is almost universal: in companies, in relationships, in child-rearing and in ourselves. We ourselves have learned to put ourselves under pressure, to reproach ourselves and kick ourselves with our guilty consciences. The kick, of course, hits the inner saboteur, who howls and plans revenge.

## Strategy 2: Carrot

Here, motivation works as follows. You hold a carrot in front of the donkey's nose, let it nibble a bit and then walk on, waving the carrot. The donkey naturally follows, hoping to get some more of the treat. Occasionally, it has to succeed or else this method won't work any more, in the short or long term! This motivational method uses *rewards, bonuses, perks, promotion, praise, recognition, flattery and pats on the head.* It's also used successfully by bosses, partners, parents—and we use it ourselves. We don't just use it with other people; we use it for ourselves too. As a reward for sticking to a diet, we allow ourselves (and our inner saboteur) a really good meal out!

"K.I.T.A." or "Carrot"-type motivators, however, both work only superficially and each has a considerable disadvantage.

*Pressure alone won't achieve motivation for the long term.* As soon as you stop kicking, the donkey will stand still. If you stop checking his homework, your son soon won't do it any more. If the new boss no longer takes action against unpunctuality, many employees will drop their previously punctual timekeeping. And we too will soon stop mainly sensible activities if we can only be motivated by pressure. You can rely on your inner saboteur one hundred percent to arrange that! We know it well: the greater the pressure, the more the little saboteur will bite. You can of course keep it in check for a while by keeping up the pressure on yourself. But the moment you slacken off it will escape. And before this stage it will use all the other tricks at its disposal to sabotage us. So none of this has much to do with true motivation.

*Even rewards lose their motivational power after a while.* There is a limit to the number of carrots you can supply—there comes a point when the donkey has had enough to eat. Surveys in the business world are all in agreement that the work mentality of sluggish and unmotivated sales personnel cannot be improved long-term by bonuses and extra commission schemes, be they ever so well thought out. Those who work only for the money will find little pleasure or satisfaction in work and will try after working hours to catch up on the life they have "missed out on". Let's assume that you reward yourself for every visit to the gym with a glass of wine in an attractive bar that you don't allow yourself to visit that often. Your little saboteur, who is mainly a hedonist by nature, will perhaps allow itself to be lulled in the early stages and allow you to go to the gym. But it will soon get used to it and will then torpedo your fitness program with excuses—unless you offer it champagne. And even that will only work for a while ...

**Pressure and reward *alone* do not have a real long-term effect on motivation.**

It's not that easy to fool your inner saboteur. However, it's been dealt a bad hand for dealing with double strategies such as the following—or even, if you get the mixture right, no excuses at all!

## *A pincer campaign for your inner saboteur*

In his book, *Descartes' Error*, Antonio R. Damasio deals in detail with the way the human brain works and the factors that have a decisive influence on our decisions. According to the results of research done in recent decades, he reports, both *pleasure and pain* play decisive parts in our choice of strategies.

**The human internal "preference system" has two primary goals in sight: *avoiding pain* and *seeking out potential pleasures*.**

Now just ask your inner saboteur what *its* primary goal is— without of course letting it into the cockpit of your inner preference system!

The pleasure and pain principle, as American motivational psychologists call it, is described by the personality trainer Alexander

Christiani in his book *Weck den Sieger in Dir!* [Wake Up the Winner Inside You]. He describes it as a "bipolar drive" (also used by advertising to manipulate us from morning till night), and he writes:

> "Advertising is basically structured as a pincer campaign. 'How bad life would be without our product, and how well off you'd be with all the advantages we offer you …' This kind of advertising is so efficient because it works in the same way as our brains.
>
> If in some area of life you are very motivated, disciplined and consistent, this is because your bipolar drive has got you in its pincer campaign. If you are motivated to do something on a regular basis (running, for example), you don't just feel good once you've done it, you very quickly feel bad if you have to do without this activity on occasion (if, for example, you have to miss your beloved cross-country run two or three times). The same principle applies to disciplined gardeners, runners, stamp collectors, readers and anyone else in this position …"

So two things are required to mount a loving but effective pincer campaign against your little saboteur:

1. Think of the *gain* the behavior you are striving for will bring. Imagine in detail how satisfying it will be and how good it will feel if you pull yourself together and perhaps even take missing out on some temporary pleasures into account.
2. Also think clearly about the *disadvantages* that will occur if you give up on your plan. Imagine, as intensely as you can, how bad you will feel later on if you give up now.

Let's assume that you have just read Karen Kingston's book *Clear Your Clutter with Feng Shui* and are now thinking about clearing the junk out of your home. You've now got enough information to picture, on the one hand, the extra space you would gain, how much more comfortable you would feel in your home, how much blocked-up energy you would release and how many other advantages this course of action would bring. On the other hand, you will realize how much energy will remain blocked, how much psychological stress would be caused by remaining surrounded by so much old junk, and what other serious effects your current state of untidiness will have on your life. If you really sit down and call up these images in detail, no little saboteur could possibly prevent your planned clear-out. On the contrary, it will help you—because you'll be having fun, and it likes to have fun too!

Experience tells us that the second stage (imagining the disadvantages) is psychologically even more important. As the whole of our nervous system is primarily oriented towards survival, the following applies:

**Our brains will do more to avoid pain than to gain pleasure and enjoyment.**

Christiani (*Weck den Sieger in Dir!*) provides a good example:

> "The difference between a true 'desk clearer' and a notorious slob is less the good feeling that both of them probably link with tidiness. It lies rather in the rapid rise of the pain curve of the tidy person. Those who can't stand mess will tidy up. The slob's mountain of work, however, will have to grow to about four feet high before enough pain gathers to lead to the insight that it's now time to tidy up."

From this point of view, all we can do is ask *which is the lesser of two evils*: carrying out the plan or not? So:

- How unpleasant would it be for me to fill in my tax return right now?
- How unpleasant would it be for me if I were to postpone filling in my tax return yet again?

Generally speaking, your inner saboteur will understand these questions, and as it is also programmed on the *bipolar principle*, it is quite possible that it will leave you in peace to fill out your tax return.

However, if it does sabotage you, there are as a rule two main reasons:

1. Either the unpleasant feelings were stronger than the pleasant ones when you imagined the results of your plan, or
2. The alternative procedure (which you should have avoided) has more pleasant than unpleasant associations.

Then of course it is you who have drawn the short straw in the struggle with your little enemy. And if both reasons are true, then don't even bother reporting for duty! In the long term, of course, even the most placid of little saboteurs won't want to be subjected to a pincer campaign. The bipolar *pleasure and pain drive* may help to get you started, to get moving or to keep going and stay on the ball in moments of weakness. However, motivation for the long term comes from within, *from enjoying the task for its own sake.* And our little saboteur likes to enjoy itself too. So what makes up the enjoyment of a task?


## "Flow" or "Find Happiness with your Saboteur"

Have you never asked yourself how it is that thousands of tennis players, footballers, surfers, mountaineers, chess players, musicians—the list goes on—have invested so much time and money in their highly motivated pursuit of their hobby? It's simple, you might reply—it's fun! True enough, but what *exactly* makes up the fun has for a long time repeatedly concerned motivational psychologists.

One man above all has dedicated himself to this question; Mihaly Csikzentmihalyi, author of the book *Flow: The Psychology of Optimal Experience.* He seems to have found the key to answering this question, and he arrives at a conclusion that is initially, perhaps, somewhat surprising. *One of the most important factors in the enjoyment of anything is challenge.* A second factor is, however, the deciding one: *The challenge must be balanced against one's own abilities.* Otherwise, matters can take a nasty turn.

What does this mean? Three scenarios can be imagined, and they are here represented by a "mathematical" equation:

Challenge > abilities = excessive demand = frustration and stress
Challenge < abilities = too little demand = boredom
Challenge = abilities = fun, excitement = flow

An example of the first equation:

A windsurfer is on his surfboard in a bay in a Force 2 wind. The wind is just right for his surfing abilities, he is having fun, he is in a good mood that day and, over-confident, he rapidly sails out of the bay into the open sea. There, however, the

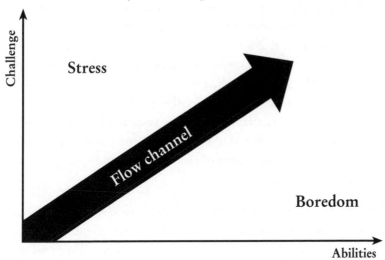

weather is quite different, with a Force 5 wind. He is soon thrown into the water and fails in all his attempts to raise the sail once more. As he and his board are driven further and further out from the shore, he must realize that, with his surfing skills, he hasn't a chance. The challenge, compared with his abilities, is far too great. The result is extreme stress and fear up to panic level.

This story did in fact happen to me some ten years ago in Greece, though it did have a happy ending, as a Greek fisherman had been watching me and pulled me out of the water. Until he turned up, however, my inner saboteur became more and more panic-stricken, and afterwards it almost never let me on a surfboard again. In the same resort, however, there were some real surf aces. They didn't get onto their boards unless there was a Force 6 or 7 wind. They would have found being on the water in a light wind boring, because the challenge, compared to their abilities, would have been far too low.

Yet another example:

When playing tennis, you would presumably have the most fun playing somebody just about as good as you, maybe just a touch better, so that sometimes one and sometimes the other would win and games continued to be exciting. If you were a considerably worse player, this would probably make you feel stressed and frustrated in the long run (unless your partner, to do you a favor, played at your level). If, however, you were very much better, boredom would be assured. So as not to lose your enjoyment of tennis, you would soon have to find another partner.

This means that only when *the challenge meets your own abilities* can you really *enjoy* something. In this way we are pushed to our limits, and yet the challenge is not too great. Then we can experience the excitement that Csikzentmihalyi describes as "flow".

### Too great and too small a challenge—the two biggest motivation killers in our lives!

This often intoxicating *flow*, this *feeling of happiness* is most often experienced when we approach or just step beyond our own limits. This applies to mountain climbing, skiing or surfing just as much as to playing music or our jobs. You will soon give up a task that in the long term presents you with too great or too small a challenge—or your little saboteur will win! But tasks and problems that challenge you and that you can solve using your abilities give the necessary spice to your working days.

In today's "mega-performance" society, with its constant demands that we go "higher, faster, further", it's more important for most people to be conscious of their own limits, and not constantly to overstrain themselves up to the point of *burnout*. One of the purposes of our little inner slacker is to warn us of such burnout. This happens gently at first but, if we won't listen and keep on pushing ourselves, it will become aggressive and pull all the sabotaging tricks it has available. If you continue to keep on working "in the red zone", it won't let you up out of your TV armchair in the evenings, or it'll have you letting off steam in a bar, and next morning all your good intentions of going for a run will be forgotten ...

Of course, we also meet our little saboteur at the "healthy" limits of challenge, and here too we have to master ourselves (and it), but rather as we would master a training partner in sport. Your little saboteur likes to play (as you can see from its character profile on page 106). Play with it, tease it, challenge it, yes, even train with it. Every day, do some little saboteur exercises, where you overcome your reluctance just a bit. From time to time, you can do a more serious exercise (further details of little saboteur training can be found from page 190 onwards). This could even be fun, as long as you don't overstrain yourself—then you'll lose out to the little saboteur. The better you get, the sooner it too will proceed to the advanced courses in the school for saboteurs. Don't worry, the game will never end. Your inner saboteur will grow with you, its tricks will become more and more sophisticated the more deliberate and skilled you yourself become. But if this didn't happen, the fun would be over. A life-long game, then! Not a bad prospect, is it? The formula is as follows:

**Avoid too small a challenge, always seek out (new) challenges, but not too great a challenge!**

You can see in the diagram below how your inner saboteur's mood will change in proportion to the intensity of your challenge.

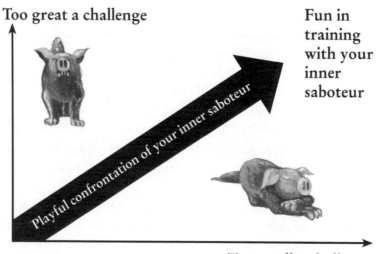

Too great a challenge

Fun in training with your inner saboteur

Playful confrontation of your inner saboteur

Too small a challenge

Your inner saboteur enjoys training too

In order to be well equipped for this training and for the playful handling of your little saboteur, you will find in the following chapter the most important strategies and means of realizing your intentions. If the inner saboteurs undergo training, it must be time to acquire the necessary equipment to confront them on an even footing!

# 8
## STRATEGIC EQUIPMENT IN FIVE STEPS

Oh no, it's those words again! The hackles are rising on your inner saboteur (and maybe you are also feeling irritated). Another self-help book is promising maximum success in five, eight or ten steps. Just a whiff of such "recipe books" is enough to have your little saboteur on the lookout, grinning as it works out its plan of defence. It knows from many years of experience that most "Easy Steps to X" self-help books leave a very important factor out of their calculations—the inner saboteur! Of course it will win again—easy!

And yet, with all due understanding for your opinion, and all due respect for your companion, you simply can't do without *strategic equipment* in this case—whether your inner companion likes it or not. Please explain, if it starts to throw a tantrum or sulk, that this time everything will be quite different—and we really do mean this seriously—as the following strategy has been devised by people who are overwhelmingly of a saboteur-friendly turn of mind, and who, as well as they can, have taken into account its psychographic structure. The aim is not to drive the little saboteur away, to lock it up or vanquish it. Our strategy is, in a manner of speaking, "saboteur-proof" in a well-intentioned way.

Here is a summary of the *five strategic steps*:

> **1.** Make a *definite decision*.
> **2.** Draw up a *clear plan of your goals*.
> **3.** Begin *putting them into practice*.
> **4.** *Monitor* your *interim results*.
> **5.** Reward yourself for your *success*.

The first three steps are the most important initially. The decisive "three steps to success" are D–P–A:

**D** ecision

**P** lanning

**A** ction

But these steps alone are not enough. The following points are also important:

- You decide WHETHER you are going to act at all:
- You plan WHAT you are going to do WHEN
- You know HOW you are going to start and follow through—and you do it!

Of course you mustn't forget to *monitor the results of the stages you have covered* or to *celebrate your successes* in an appropriate manner. However, once you have *really decided, planned properly*, and then taken the *first step*, you little foe has only a very small chance of crossing you as the program continues.

## STEP 1: THE DEFINITE DECISION

The success of a plan stands or falls according to the *definite nature of the decision*. Many intentions that have soon fallen victim to our inner saboteur had no chance from the beginning, because we didn't really want to carry them out in the first place and therefore only made a *half-hearted resolution* (you can find out where the flaw lies in a decision in Chapter 2, from page 54 on). In order not to create any more stillborn intentions, the best way is to proceed as follows:

If you have not done so already, please draw up a list of all the things you have intended to do—maybe for a long time—and have always put off but now want to do them at last or at least make a start. Separate one-off activities (such as clearing out the basement, going to the dentist for a checkup) from long-term changes in behavior (such as daily time planning, losing weight, regular fitness training). On page 136 you will find a list that could serve as an example.

You could of course make two separate lists for one-off actions and changes to behavior. In the example on page 136, we have simply noted plans in the order in which they might occur. You could also distinguish between larger or more difficult, and smaller or easier plans. However, formulating your plan exactly is not, at this point, essential. It could of course happen that your inner saboteur starts to smile when once again you want to "read more books". But let it smile—by the next stage at the latest you will have made a practical plan.

For each point on your list, make a conscious decision as to whether you are really going to act on it—or whether you are going to put the plan on ice (at least for a time). Have the courage to say no to some things if you find that you really won't have any time for them or actually don't want to put the plan into practice. You could for instance realize that making a garden pond is not possible, either financially or in time terms, this year—even if your brother has just made a medium-sized puddle for his inner saboteur in his garden. There might as yet be no time this year for the dance course, and the global positioning system for your car is also more of a non-essential toy.

| All the things I've been wanting to do | | |
|---|---|---|
| Plan | One-off action | Changes in behavior |
| Hanging up pictures on stairs | x | |
| Clearing out garage | x | |
| Sorting books in basement | x | |
| Evaluating and throwing out magazines | x | |
| Preparing tax return | x | |
| Sorting out conflict with neighbors | x | |
| Dentist checkup | x | |
| Lose at least 20lbs | | xx |
| Go for regular runs | | xx |
| Dance course with Monica | | x |
| Go to the theater/to concerts more often | | x |
| Read more books/watch less TV | | x |
| Sort out finances | x | |
| Acquire global positioning system for car | x | |
| Learn a foreign language | | x |
| Apply to work abroad | x | |
| Visit Richard in hospital | x | |
| Plan summer holidays | x | |
| Set up time schedule on computer | | x |

For most of the points, you will be able to make a very quick and definite decision, especially for one-off actions. However, with plans that you have put off for some time and where you are in doubt as to whether you really want to decide on them (finally) at all—in particular planned changes in behavior—it would be best to draw up a list of advantages and disadvantages of action (or inaction). You can use this summary, if necessary, to mount a loving but firm emotional pincer campaign (following the pleasure and pain principle) against your inner saboteur.

| Evaluating advantages and disadvantages of action (or inaction) | |
| --- | --- |
| **Action** | **Inaction** |
| What advantages would I gain if I finally start on my Plan X and put it into practice?<br>• What would the foreseeable situation be in a year's time?<br>• And what about in a month's time? | What would be the disadvantages if I don't start on my Plan X and continue to postpone it?<br>• What would the foreseeable situation be in a year's time?<br>• And if I continue on this course, how would things look in 10, 20 or 30 years' time? |
| What disadvantages could be linked to action? | What, in contrast, would be the advantages if I don't act or continue with my present course of behavior? |
| Do the advantages of action clearly outweigh the disadvantages? | Do the advantages of inaction clearly outweigh the disadvantages? |

In some cases, where our little opponent has been very obstinate in its struggles against a necessary change in our habits, only an unsparing analysis and forcing ourselves to be conscious of what we are doing to ourselves and where this is leading can wake us up and suddenly arouse the will to change.

Sonia, one of the students taking part in a seminar, lived in a house she had inherited. Unfortunately, though, it stood at a crossroads with a great deal of traffic noise and such powerful exhaust emissions that she couldn't hang the washing out to dry in the garden, or it would turn black. On the other hand, it was her grandparents' house—and it didn't cost her anything. Anywhere else, she would have to pay considerably more for a comparable house than she would get from selling her present one. Her "inheritance" was also in serious need of renovation, but she took no steps to arrange for this, as she was not sure she would continue to live there. This was a dilemma crying out for a solution, but for almost five years she had put off a decision again and again. Sometimes, her little saboteur suggested, "You can't do this to your family—sell your grandparents' house!" At other times, it tried the "You need to get some proper information first" approach. Then again, it would try "It's not that important, after all." Or it would simply employ the reluctance to act tactics. In the seminar, Sonia needed fewer than 20 minutes to draw up her list of advantages and disadvantages. Her inner saboteur shut up at once. The decision was clear. Sonia's list looked something like this:

| Sonia's evaluation of the advantages and disadvantages of action (inaction) | |
| --- | --- |
| Action | Inaction |
| *Advantages* of selling the house and moving ... <br><br> ... in a year's time <br> • No traffic noise <br> • No exhaust gases <br> • Less stress <br> • Healthier life <br> • Feeling good <br> • I'd know where I belong <br> • Lots of unnecessary junk and superfluous furniture would be got rid of (= less ballast) <br><br> ... in a month's time <br> • No more hesitation <br> • Clarity about what I want <br> • I can act | *Disadvantages* of not selling ... <br><br> ... in a year's time <br> • Continuing lack of clarity <br> • Continuing stress with noise and exhaust emissions <br> • Guilty conscience <br> • Not much pleasure in living in a shabby house <br> • Less energy than ever <br><br> ... in 10, 20, 30 years' time: <br> • Unthinkable to go on living like this! <br> • Horrible! <br> • What a nightmare! <br> (By this point at the latest it is clear what she wants!) |

| Sonia's evaluation of the advantages and disadvantages of action (inaction) (continued) | |
|---|---|
| **Action** | **Inaction** |
| • Prospect of change<br>• Doing something for me<br>• Looking forward to change<br>• New start | |
| *Disadvantages:*<br>• Leaving the old house<br>• Limited to a smaller house or apartment<br>• Time investment | *Advantages:*<br>• No need to act (nothing else!) |
| *Conclusion:*<br>Advantages clearly outweigh disadvantages | *Conclusion:*<br>Disadvantages outweigh advantages—no contest! |

Two months after drawing up this list she had sold the house and moved—accompanied of course by her little saboteur—into a much smaller but quieter two-bedroom apartment in a park environment.

In this phase of evaluation and coming to a decision, use the *R–K–W principle*. In other words,

R eally

K now

W hy

This is how the principle functions: there are many occasions when we don't change things because we don't know what change will bring. We are not clear about *why* we want to do something or how much our previous behavior has been damaging us. Here we need to act: *get the necessary information from the experts*, from books, seminars, lectures, films or other sources of information such as the internet. Medical health checks (even if your little companion grumbles) are of course also part of the information-gathering process.

Most often, we not only don't know *why*, we also avoid making any decisions on changes because we don't really know *how* to change things. Whether it's learning to handle a computer, dancing, losing weight or running—we often think before we do anything that it's bound to be much too complicated, too strenuous, that we will have to give up too much or that it will take up too much time (all of this, of course, is ammunition for the little saboteur)—until someone has explained it or shown us how to do it and we have then done it. With the wisdom of experience, we can then say, "It really isn't very difficult, on the contrary, it's much simpler and less hard work than I thought. If only I'd known that before!" How often in your life have you told yourself the above? And how often do you want to say it again? Get all the necessary information from the experts and find out *how to do it as simply as possible*—then your inner saboteur won't come up with any more devastating arguments!

Make the decision easier by really knowing the *why* and the *how*.

## Step 2: Set Definite Goals

*"Would you tell me, please, which way I ought to walk from here?" Alice in Wonderland asks the Cheshire Cat, after meeting it at a crossroads. "That depends a great deal on where you want to get to," the Cat replies. "I don't much care where," says Alice. The Cat responds with the simple statement, "Then it doesn't matter which way you walk."*

Looking at almost any diary, you would think of Seneca's matchless remark: *No wind is the right wind for those who do not know their harbor.*

If you have *no goals*, you're unlikely to have trouble with your little saboteur. If you have no "harbor" to steer for, and if you don't care where you come ashore, you might as well leave your saboteur in charge of the helm ... No, your inner saboteur will pop up *when* you have goals—and of course you have them now, as a consequence of having made a definite decision. It is essential now to secure your chosen goals by *definite planning* against any possible attacks by your little foe. This will be easiest if you take into account, as far as possible, the way your command center, in other words your brain, works. The more *realistic, precise and deadline-bound* your inner goals are, the weaker your little saboteur's resistance will become! Good intentions that want to survive (and not be eaten up) necessarily have the five following (brain-friendly) characteristics. They are:

- realistic and performable
- positively worded
- measurable in practical terms
- given fixed deadlines
- given a clear image of the goal.

## *Realistic and performable*

You know the sort of good advice friends and acquaintances give. "That's not difficult." "You can do that!" "It would be ridiculous if *you* couldn't manage that!" "All you need to do is make an effort!" Such advice (however well-meant) usually does you very little good if *you* have the feeling that you can't make it or at least that it would cost you too great an effort. Sometimes such advice can even get you down. "All you need to do is pull yourself together!" is what we hear at home, and all I can reply is, "That's what you think!" If that was *all*, the neighborhood should be full of healthy, fit, successful people with no problems in overcoming their little saboteurs (if the saboteurs were still around and hadn't all emigrated long ago).

Of course, goals can only be *realistic* if they fall within the limits of our *objective* abilities and capacities, and are therefore not too (measurably and demonstrably) great a challenge. If, at 40 years of age, a non-swimmer planned to win the gold medal at the next Olympic Games for the 100m butterfly stroke, it would be obvious to anyone that such a plan was outside that person's abilities and capacities. We, however,will only see a plan as realistic if it *appears performable to us*; in other words, if it lies within our *subjectively* experienced capacities. This is one of the most delicate points in our dealings with our inner saboteur. You must consider this aspect (and your saboteur) when setting your goals, you must take it into account, or your little opponent will sabotage it by all available means. And I'd bet money on it—it will succeed! If in setting your goals (however good your intentions) you set the bar too high, it will before very long considerably raise your inner inhibitions. And you'll soon get that unpleasant "I'll never make it" feeling, and a well-known inner voice will whisper, "Of course you can't make it! No one could!"

Why are so many people unable to put their good intentions, such as "From tomorrow I'll stop smoking", "I'll lose 40 pounds", "At last I'll clear out the whole house, including basement, attic and garage" into practice? Because the unnerving feeling creeps up on them in advance: "I'll never make it!" Your project then stands before you like a huge, insurmountable psychological mountain, and your inner saboteur (with the very best of intentions) will do all it can to remove these threatening, upsetting, unperformable plans. Once they have given up their project, most people feel better for a while— at least as far as that distressing feeling is concerned. That's enough for your inner saboteur, which after all lives mainly in the present.

If we want to put a large-scale plan into practice—without putting ourselves under massive pressure and constantly having to battle our then extremely aggressive and ill-tempered little saboteur—there is only one way:

## We need to feel in advance that our plan is performable.

We need to feel, "I can do that!" or "That really can be done!" You can achieve this feeling by, on the one hand, informing yourself and getting the necessary information as to the simplest way of starting on your plan, and on the other by breaking it up into *small stages or units*. Because:

## Big ideas are more easily put into practice in small stages!

This is the secret of the *mini-max principle*. Mini-stages accumulate to make maximum success. To apply the mini-max principle you can differentiate as follows, according to your chosen goal:

**Small matters that you put off** that can easily be done in a *one-off action* (such as hanging up those pictures, opening a bank account, that visit to the doctor, that long overdue letter) should be approached *like eating oysters*. Just as you eat one oyster after another, act on one plan after another—and never do two things at once.

In other words, never fight on two fronts at the same time. The best way is to spread out the postponed plans on your list *one at a time* to different days over a longer period of time, and then, for example, attack *one* plan a day every day. Or, if it makes more sense, *combine* several plans and do all of these on a single day in one go—but even here, do them one after the other. To take one example, combine your visit to the doctor with doing a few errands afterwards.

**Larger matters** that you are unlikely to manage in one go, which on the contrary require *more time and perseverance* (such as clearing out and renovating the whole basement, learning a new language, preparing for an exam, planning a project, reading a book) should be like eating elephants. You cut the elephant into small pieces and eat it bit by bit.

THE LITTLE SABOTEUR

This saying, which comes from India, is often described as the *salami technique*. This means that:

**Just as you cut a salami into thin slices, divide a large project into *small, manageable and time-limited units*, and then attack these *in small stages*.**

Such an approach lowers the level of inhibition about starting, and makes beginning a project easier if the motivation is not all it should be—and motivation will grow with every small, partial success. Even small stages can have a big effect. In this way you can also trick your inner saboteur, as it tends to overlook small matters and small plans. It won't resent your doing this—it really isn't that small-minded. And another extra piece of advice: *When in doubt, take smaller rather than bigger "bites" at the beginning!*

Of course, it's not very motivating if you set yourself too small a challenge, but you can always increase the amount that you do. The main thing is to have the feeling "I can do this" and not to be prevented from starting.

> Robert was standing in the bookshop. In one hand he held a self-help book on planning your finances. Yes indeed, he had wanted to get around to doing so for a long time, but already his invisible companion was saying, "When are you going to read that? 220 pages! You've got enough to do as it is. Anyway, it's all dry stuff. You can't relax, reading that." Robert had almost put the book back on the shelf when he remembered the elephant rule and made some quick calculations: "Five pages a day Monday to Friday (while on the train to work), Saturdays and Sundays ten pages a day, adds up to 45 pages a week, a total of five weeks—yes, I can do that!" And because he had the feeling that he would be able to do it in this manner, his little saboteur shut up. Even it was convinced. It almost carried the book home for Robert.

**Changes to behavior**, where you want to enrich your life long-term by acquiring a *new habit* (planning your schedule for the day, regular sport, new, healthier ways of eating or "only" allowing yourself a short break every day to refresh yourself) can be approached using the same principle—small stages, especially at the beginning, small units. It's better to run for ten minutes a day than have your inner saboteur shoot down your good intentions in flames. Making a habit out of a new behavior pattern—however sensible it might be—brings its own particular problems and is therefore one of the good intentions that most often becomes the victim of the inner saboteur. However, if the details are known, even these problems can easily be mastered. Which is why this most important topic has its own chapter (see page 165).

*Conclusion:* To make an effort, you need the feeling of performability. When setting your goals, therefore (whatever these goals may be), keep asking yourself these decisive questions: "How can I arrange things so that this plan seems performable for me?" "What can I do to make the start, the first step, easier for me?" The decisive piece of information in dealing with your inner saboteur is this:

**To make the effort, you need that feeling
of performability.**

## Positive wording

So many of our good intentions have no chance of survival right from the start, because they don't correspond to the way our brains work. A majority of these are all those occasions when we tell ourselves—however firmly—that we are going to do something "less often" or "not any more". Our brains can't imagine this. You can't "not think" something—however hard you try. And what you can't imagine is very hard to put into practice (more details in the section on page 154, *A brightly lit goal and an inner film*).

Just try it for yourself. I now give you an express instruction not to think of a black cat.

No, you must have misunderstood me—I said *not* to think of a black cat! The problem is that this is the very thing that won't work. My instruction is not "brain-friendly", just like the sign in the camper belonging to the well-known management trainer Vera F. Birkenbihl:

> **Please**
> **Do NOT**
> **Read this sign**

The term "brain-friendly" also originates with Vera F. Birkenbihl. Anything that isn't "brain-friendly" you can forget about—often quite literally. How can your brain help you if it cannot *positively*, that is to say actually, imagine what you want? What does it look like when you resolve "not to work so much any more", "not to lose your temper so quickly", "not to smoke so much any more"? The moment you try to put this into words you will of necessity have to say what you would be doing *instead*. It may not be possible to imagine *no* black cat, but it is possible to imagine an empty space (in which, *automatically*, there is no black cat because the space is empty). This is the way to word a brain-friendly resolution. On the one hand, it expresses what you want to do instead (for instance, "go home earlier to play with the children" (instead of "work less"). On the other hand, it sets down *precisely* what you want to do instead, so you can avoid falling straight into the next trap of unmeasurable "wishy-washy wording"—read more about it in the next section. (So please make *exact* resolutions, such as that you'll go home every day from now on at five-thirty instead of six o'clock, in order to play with your children—when wording your intention, follow the examples below).

| How to word resolutions positively and exactly | | |
|---|---|---|
| Negative wording | Positive wording | Exact wording |
| "Work less" | "Go home earlier" | "Go home every day at 5 o'clock" |
| "Not to lose my temper" | "React quietly and calmly" | "Take three deep breaths before reacting" |
| "Smoke less" | "Smoke only a limited number of cigarettes" | "Smoke a maximum of five cigarettes a day" |
| "Not to eat so unhealthily any more" | "Eat more healthily" | "Only buy organic products etc." |

And please remember, along with your positive and exact wording, to express your *decision*, so as not to fall into the trap of "eternally trying" (see Chapter 2, page 54). So don't say "I will *try* to go home every day at 5 o'clock from now on", but "I want to/I will …" This means that your little saboteur has fewer chances of swallowing your good intentions as a tasty snack.

## Exact and measurable

How can a mail order company deliver if it receives no exact order? Your brain can't carry out your instructions if you just order "more" or "less" of something. (We have already shown, in describing the blurring tactics of the little saboteurs, why such commands in the comparative don't work). How would you know, anyway, if you have reached your goal? How would you know if you have finally managed to do "more" for your health?

To put it plainly: *What can't be measured can't be demonstrated!* So:

**Set yourself clearly worded, measurable goals.**

The more *precise* your goals, the less chance your inner saboteur has of tricking you or blurring your purpose. On the contrary, in such cases it will often not even try to interfere with your plans. If the challenge your exact and measurable intention sets you is not too great, because, for example, you are learning only ten new items of vocabulary a day in a foreign language, it won't think things are so bad (because they are "performable") and will let you learn in peace while it takes a nap, safe in the knowledge that there's no danger of its owner taking on too much, at only ten words a day. (Though after three months you'll know some 900 words, the basic vocabulary of a language!)

## *Fixed dates in writing*

"No date—no love!" Those in love arrange to meet. They don't wait to see if they accidentally run across their beloved by chance somewhere or other. They agree on a fixed time at a certain place. And it's fairly unlikely that one of the two will put off his or her beloved.

Your "beloved" is your intention. Do the same, make a "date" with it, or your "affair" won't stand much of a chance. If you really love your intention and believe in it from the bottom of your heart, then you'll do it, and the driving force will be your desire to put it into practice. Your little saboteur won't have many arguments against a fixed "date"—if you like going to this "date" and if it is sensible and can be done.

**You want to go running? Not without your little saboteur!**

Without a fixed "date", you probably wouldn't get out of bed in the morning. "Why?" your little saboteur whispers. "Come on, let's sleep a bit more, it's so comfortable in bed." "No, I've got a date!" "Really?" "Yes, I want to go for a run." "You don't say! You won't do too much?" "Only 20 minutes. It'll be really good for me and I feel like it too." "OK, go and have your run, I'll sleep a bit longer. Wake me when you've got some more interesting plans, I'm beginning to get hungry !"

**Fixed dates are essential for putting your plans into practice. Without dates, all power lies in the hands of your saboteur.**

For larger projects approached according to the salami technique, don't just set a fixed *final date* or so-called *deadline*. Set *interim dates* as well, up to which you want to have achieved fixed stages of your goal, and *individual dates* for every day. For me as a student, for example, it's a great help if I go to my desk and know that now, from 10.15 to 11.00, I'll be learning only the material on pages 185 to 198 in textbook X. If my plan and my tasks for the day are clear to me in the morning, it's much easier for me to get up. And another tip—don't just plan in your head, but *write down your times and dates* in your personal organizer, diary or calendar, just as you would any other business appointment.

Here are a few well-tried tips for inoculating your times and dates against any possible attacks from your inner saboteur:

**Plan in extra time and buffer zones.** Estimate the time necessary for a particular plan and reserve *at least one-third more time*, in some cases even twice the time. Experience shows that we often tend to seriously underestimate how long things will take. It's only too easy to believe that clearing out the basement will take one day at most. I ask you: in which of these two situations are you more satisfied with yourself? If, at the end of the Saturday you have reserved to clear out the depths of your cellar, you have to admit that you've only managed half of it, or if you've added Sunday as a buffer zone to your plans and then discover that against all expectations you've actually cleared 80 percent of it on the evening of the first day? I suspect that the second situation could motivate you so strongly that you'll be enthusiastically working on your basement till two in the morning, and then spending Sunday suitably celebrating your victory over chaos!

**Plan enough breaks and free time.** If you don't plan for any breaks or allow yourself any free time to regenerate, relax and enjoy, you'll not only soon be working at half charge and with little enjoyment, but you'll also be struggling with your little inner slacker, trying to sabotage your efforts by all means at its disposal. If however you have allowed for enough "air" and free time, your saboteur will have no real reason to put the brakes on. This too needs to be planned. Such free time doesn't come of its own accord, especially with "long haul workers". Neil Fiore, author of the anti-procrastination manual *The Now Habit*, even recommends starting your planning for the week with your leisure time. A crazy idea, you think? But just right for your little saboteur. Just try it! Your little saboteur will happily support you in your scheduling (which before you had so often put off ...)

**Plan in rewards.** Once you have attained the goal (or interim goal), allow yourself something nice or pleasant as a reward—a bottle of champagne, a visit to the cinema, buying some nice clothes, eating in a good restaurant or even, if a larger plan is involved, a trip to Paris with your partner. Say it (and write it down): "Once I've filled in my tax return, I'll allow myself an afternoon at the spa with a massage." Looking forward to your treat will *motivate* you, not just *on your way* to your goal. Planning also increases the chances that you *really will be celebrating* and giving yourself the reward, instead of starting off on the way to the next goal or just dropping back into daily routine.

**Give Priority Number One as early as the planning stage to all plans where you have to reckon on opposition from your inner saboteur.** As in motor racing, have your plan start in "pole position". Any problems with your inner saboteur are best sorted in this privileged position *right at the start of the day*, when you have the best inner and time resources. It doesn't matter whether it's the daily run of events or replying to a difficult letter. The experience of success will also speed you on your way for dealing with the other tasks of the day in a quite different manner than thinking all day about the appointment you still have with your little saboteur. If you simply can't find time in the morning, reserve some other "protected time" for your plan, perhaps not until the evening or the weekend. But remember that it's better to drop something (if it's not essential for your private or professional life) than to give up a saboteur problem because of time pressure. In other words, saboteur problems have priority!

> Jill, a student in one of my seminars, reported how she had suffered from her disinclination to write letters. She was forever battling with "letter debt", and her saboteur seemed to be using all possible excuses to prevent her from writing so much as a postcard. The mountain of unanswered correspondence grew higher and higher, and her little saboteur found it easy to stick the "I can't possibly manage that lot" label on it. At the height of her dissatisfaction, she decided to solve the problem in small stages: to write to one person every day, even if it was no more than a postcard with the words "Thinking of you! Jill"—and to do this first thing in the morning. For six months she gave this plan number one priority, and then it had become so much a matter of course that she would even write a letter during a break in her day. Once she had begun, the letters often grew to be quite long. Yes, she did indeed write 365 letters and postcards

in a year. Her saboteur seemed hardly to have noticed. Perhaps it was still so sleepy in the mornings that it was unable to protest. It was this trick of giving small "bites" of new plans priority one that became the key for her to change several things in her life.

**Give your plan some presence.** If you really want to make a saboteur problem into an affair of the heart, give it *presence*! Try and remind yourself of an important plan as often as possible during the day. Mark the entry with highlighter in your diary, stick notes in all possible places (in your notebook, in the car, on your suitcase, in your wallet, on the phone, in the bathroom or the kitchen) or put up a notice above your desk or bed. If a change in behavior that will enrich your life is involved, it's often helpful to read a book on the topic. For instance, a book on healthy eating can provide support at a time when you want to lose weight. Another good method is to set up a figure symbolizing your plan. In brief, the more present your intentions are in your thinking (but please don't get fixated on them!) the less success your inner saboteur will have in simply letting you forget what you actually wanted to do.

Here follows a summary of the essential points:

1. Make dates in writing! And set yourself *individual dates*, *interim dates* and *final dates*.
2. Support your intentions by planning in
   - *Spare time* and *buffer time*
   - *Breaks and free time*
   - *Rewards*.
3. Give your intentions *priority number one* and *presence*.

## *A brightly lit goal and an inner film*

Once you have positively worded, measurably fixed and given dates to your "performable" intentions, you will need a *clear image* of them before you can finally get going. Imagine to yourself in detail what your basement will look like once you have tidied it up. How will you feel in three months' time when you have gone running every day and have already lost 14lbs? What will it be like when you have given your top presentation and everyone has applauded? Paint in bright colors how you will feel, how relieved and proud you will be. Because:

**The brighter your image of your goal, the weaker
the resistance of your inner saboteur.**

Why is that so? We know by now that the little saboteurs are not very susceptible to rational thinking. They don't follow the intellect, but their feelings (which is why, in the struggle between intellect and feelings, feelings usually win out in the long term). And these *inner images arouse feelings*. The more radiant your image of your goal, the more positive the emotions linked to it will be—and the stronger will be the effect on you *and* your little saboteur. So remember: *the little saboteurs will be more easily won over by colorful, bright pictures than by rational arguments!*

The stronger your image of your goal, the more likely it is that it will come about. In the early years of computer development, the achievement of so-called WYSIWYG technology was a great breakthrough. WYSIWYG stands for "What you see is what you get" and means that *you get* (in the printout) *what you see* (on the screen). Today it's a matter of course, but then it was a great step forward. Our brains work in much the same way: WYSIWYG

The "bitesize" way to success—even your little saboteur
will be pleased to help!

applies here too. *What you see (in your imagination) is what you get (in your life).* These inner images determine your feelings and through them the results of your efforts. Get hold of your feelings and use them to drive your motivation forward.

Best of all, go a stage further: don't just paint a bright picture of your goal, but "shoot" an *inner film* as well; a film about *how* you are going to get to your goal, all the things you will do in detail. The more detailed the film, the better.

Have you ever seen how slalom skiers prepare for their races? Slowly and concentrating hard, they pass along the marked slalom course. Then, in the "cinema" in their minds, they imagine an inner film of themselves going down this slope and through the gates. Again and again! When they go to the starting point, they have already run the race numerous times in thought. Their entire nervous system is programmed, all they have to do is follow through physically—and their bodies will almost automatically follow the film stored inside their minds.

You can make use of this technique in everyday life by imagining, before you act, as exactly as possible all the things you will do, how you will proceed, and what, in the end, your achieved goal will look like. This technique, by the way, was a great help to me in resolving my "clear out the garage" syndrome.

When I wanted to get up at seven o'clock on that Saturday morning, I immediately noticed that there was going to be a serious struggle with my inner saboteur. It wanted at least another hour in bed. So, while I was still lying in bed, I began in my mind to clear out and tidy up the garage. I considered which items I was going to take to the tip, how I was going to pack them into the car, how I was going to sort out the other things in the garage, how I would fasten them to the walls or place them on the shelves—until I had a clear picture of the tidied-up garage before me. Once the colorful film in my head was finished, my little saboteur had lost its chance. When I started work on the clear-out an hour later, most of the work had already been done mentally. The rest was only the completion (which was also why I finished much more quickly than I had ever thought I would).

This is yet another clear example:

**The more detailed the inner film, the quicker and easier the action becomes!**

## STEP 3: PUTTING INTO PRACTICE

When putting a plan into practice, there are two *decisive moments* that are vital: one is the *start* and the other is *keeping going in the "weak moments"*. As described above, these are the two phases where our plans are particularly vulnerable to any acts of sabotage by our little inner gremlins.

### *Start at once if you can!*

The quicker you take the first step the better! The first step is the most important investment in putting your plan into practice.

The best thing is just to make a start, even quite spontaneously and without planning to, just *to get ahead of your inner saboteur*. Before the latter has really noticed what's happening, you'll have started to run and got out of reach (if only temporarily) of its objections. This first experience of success, for which you have thus laid the foundations in your nervous system, can then serve you as a defence against subsequent attacks by your inner companion.

Just like that? Yes, *just like that!* In some cases it can be a good thing to get something done, even without having an exact idea of the project, and even if this action is perhaps not perfect or represents only a small step with a long way still to go. Have the courage to be imperfect sometimes! The demand for perfect results is one of the main causes of constant postponement. In other words:

### Better to do something 80% well than 100% not to do it at all!

Just make a start! Take a spontaneous dive into the cold water. Little saboteurs like to stay on shore, they hate cold water. And if you're not "quite sure"? Try acting as if you were sure. Grab hold of the problem; you could gain some important experiences.

Make a start, even if you think you're "not really in the mood". Act, *even if you don't feel like acting.* Many people believe motivation leads to action. That may well be true, but the opposite also applies: action often leads to motivation. "Appetite comes with eating", the proverb says; especially if we find out that it's all much easier than we had thought beforehand. Action is also one of the best methods of dispelling depression and bad moods. You're not in the mood? OK, do something!

If you've also taken care when planning to ensure that making a start will be as easy as possible for you (to ensure "performability"), then it won't cost you too much effort to take the first step. And you won't have to reckon with large-scale campaigns by your little saboteur.

Of course, your saboteur, after reading the statements above, could suddenly whisper in your ear, "Hang on a minute! You can't jump in just like that! What about clearly envisaging your goal, drawing up a detailed plan with fixed dates …?" This is, in principle, true of a large-scale plan. But if you suddenly remember that you have to sort something out with a friend (something you've been putting off for a long time), and you really feel the need to get the matter cleared up at last, then it might be better and more sensible to write a letter at once or grab the phone, rather than put it off and set dates ... or you've decided to clear out your house. Good idea! Start straight away, even if you only take the first boxes of junk to the tip. You have taken the first step. You can draw up the full strategic plan in the evening, over a glass of wine or cup of tea.

> In this way Anita tamed her computer saboteur (you remember? The saboteur with all the reasons why computers and the internet were not for Anita). When she got home from the seminar, she simply switched on her laptop, had a friend briefly show her how to call up a Word document, and wrote a line, without thinking about it too much. Just like that! From then on, she wrote at least a line every day and each time learned another function as well (often more). After a few weeks, she could carry out the tasks that were most important for her on the computer—without problems. However, the real breakthrough for her was that first step— no great preparation, just switch on and write.

In brief, the formula, instead of P–D–D (Postpone, Date and Do) could in some cases be reduced to D–I–N—Do It Now!

## *Keep going and carry on!*

The danger of giving up on a plan which you have already begun really only exists for large-scale programs that, following the "salami technique", are spread over a longer period of time—or for changes to behavior where you are fighting against old habits. For the latter, there are some anti-saboteur strategies in the section "Monitoring interim results" on page 161. Here are a few general, tried and tested tips for carrying on:

**Never completely give up on a plan because of a momentary mood.** Never throw in the towel completely. At most, decide on *end of stage deadlines*, where you can think again whether or not you really want to complete a project you have begun.

Let's assume that for health reasons you want to give up meat and meat products for Lent (the time between Ash Wednesday and Easter). It could happen that after nine days a powerful desire for salami suddenly overcomes you and your inner saboteur offers all sorts of reasons why such abstinence really isn't doing any good.

In such a case, postpone the important decision as to whether you are really going to give up your resolution to the next day or to Sunday, if you have decided on Sunday as your "rethink day" (meaning the one day on which you are allowed to rethink your decision). It could be that it really isn't the right thing for you to give up meat completely for such a long time. But *decide on this rationally* and not as the result of a weak moment. Your inner saboteur is not the right adviser for such decisions.

**Practice putting up with negative feelings from time to time.** It's not necessary to flee them at once. Try simply to recognize them and still keep to your plan, without following the tempting call to do something else—however enticingly the TV calls you! If the pull becomes very strong, Hans-Werner Rückert, in his book *Schluss mit dem ewigen Aufschieben. Wie Sie umsetzen, was Sie sich vornehmen* [Stop Putting It Off: How to Put Your Plans Into Practice], recommends that you "Ask yourself whether you really *must, now* and *at once!*" Must you watch TV now, at this moment? No, it's only an excuse put forward by your little saboteur to get you out of your plan quick. Save the "sweet temptation" as a reward. Then later on you can enjoy what you would now only be doing half-heartedly, with twinges of guilty conscience.

**If things become too strenuous, move down a gear.** Slow your speed or reduce the amount you are doing, in other words cut your project into even thinner salami slices.

**Only if you really can't go on, throw the project over—but just for this one day!** If at the 17th stage everything is going wrong, your heart is down in your boots and your inner saboteur is advising you to throw in the towel, then—and only then—you can take a short "break". Go and cry on a good friend's shoulder or allow yourself a treat—but carry on the next day as if nothing had happened. Then your break wasn't falling into the "exceptions trap", it was just an interruption on a long path. In time, you will notice more and more quickly when your little saboteur tries to keep you (with justification) from overdoing things and a break is really necessary, and when it just wants to tempt you in order to eat up your good intentions.

**Don't compare yourself with others.** Many a good start has been wrecked on these particular rocks. And if you just can't avoid it, at least don't compare yourself with the wrong people.

- Don't compare yourself with those who are much better. That will *pull you down.*
- Don't compare yourself with those who give up or drop out. That will *pull you out.*
- If you must compare yourself with others (and orient yourself by their actions), then compare yourself with those who keep going and stay with the job. That will *pull you on.*

## Step 4: Monitoring Interim Results

The very best planning won't help you without *monitoring.* Monitoring, for you, will have a *double effect.* On the one hand, you will acquire some *orientation* and be able to see how far you have come with your project. You will recognize what is still to be done to achieve your goal and how you may have to adjust your plan if it should in part have turned out to be unrealistic (and don't worry: nearly every plan needs to be adjusted to circumstances from time to time). On the other hand, it will strengthen your *motivation* each time when you become conscious of the partial successes you have achieved to date. Make a note of interim results you have achieved in a "success diary" or, even better, *visualize your progress*! Write out your plan, including interim stage goals, and hang it on a pinboard. Mark your successes in color so that you can see them again and again.

Assuming that you have resolved to run regularly, then enter your daily running time into a graph. Then you can see at any time how the length of your runs is gradually increasing (as you had to make an exception on the 19th day, you went running for 15 minutes in the morning and at least another 10 minutes in the evening of the following day).

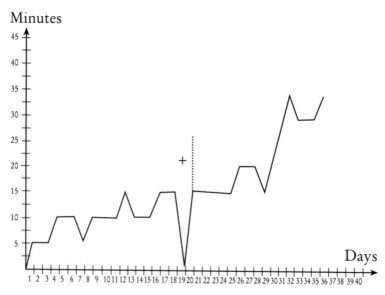

It can be even more effective in the first weeks to add up your part successes. By accumulating your individual performances, the line of the graph will rise more steeply, which can increase motivation even more, especially in the difficult early stages.

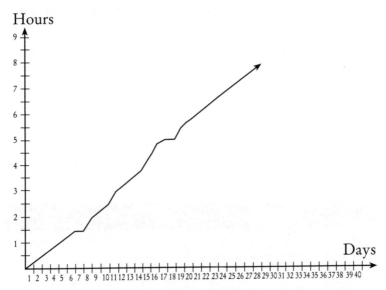

It is very satisfactory and fulfilling when you make gradual progress in areas of life where it previously cost you much effort to change or where you have repeatedly capitulated to your inner saboteur. It is good to see how you are moving forwards. Even if the steps are small, keep looking at them and use the resources of visualization. Your little saboteur will be impressed by them. Show them to it!

## Step 5: Don't Forget the Reward

Don't forget to *celebrate* when you have reached your goal—and the same applies to smaller interim stage goals. Don't ever cheat yourself out of the promised reward. Your little saboteur would take that very badly. It would never forgive you. Promises must be kept. Otherwise it really will step on the brake with your next plan. On the other hand, the more you reward yourself, the more often, for instance, you allow yourself to take a break or to relax, the more it will be inclined to leave you in peace for your next project as well. Give yourself a pat on the back, you have plenty of reason to be proud of yourself. No false modesty, please (that doesn't mean you have to become too full of yourself). The Association of Inner Saboteurs has for many years been successfully using acts of sabotage to undermine the widespread tendency to carry on immediately and sweep any successes under the carpet. A sure means to prevent them is to celebrate and reward yourself.

The table below shows a summary in five steps of the equipment described in this chapter. Now nothing can go wrong!

| Strategic equipment in five steps |
|---|
| 1. Make a definite **decision** by<br>  • making a list of all your plans<br>  • and making a conscious decision (with lists of advantages and disadvantages if required).<br><br>The essential point is to know why and how you do something. |
| 2. Prepare to start with clear **goal planning**:<br>  • Set a realistic and performable goal ("I can do that!" using small steps, little bites, making it easy to start).<br>  • Word your goal in a "brain-friendly", i.e. positive, manner.<br>  • The goal must be exactly measurable and demonstrable.<br>  • Fix dates for your goal in writing, including extra time and buffer zones, breaks and free time, rewards and, above all, priority one and presence in your life.<br>  • Create a brightly lit goal and inner film (WYSIWYG). |
| 3. Start **putting your plan into practice** right away (just like that and even if you're not in the mood) and keep going! |
| 4. **Monitor** and **visualize** your success. |
| 5. Remember to **reward** yourself and **celebrate**! |

# 9
## SPECIAL TIPS FOR
## LONG-TERM CHANGES IN BEHAVIOR

A project that requires a change in long-established patterns of behavior is often a difficult one. It's only too easy, in such circumstances, for our little saboteur to get in the way, because it really hates effort. The following will show you some tried-and-tested strategies for "muzzling" your faithful friend.

## WHY MANY PEOPLE FIND CHANGING BEHAVIOR DIFFICULT

The atmosphere in the little French bistro was good. The food was delicious. And conversation was animated and cheerful until Harry asked the fateful question: "Well, how's the new fitness lifestyle going?" Immediately, Michaela's expression darkened and she sighed.

Not quite eight weeks ago, she had, with great enthusiasm, read a book on health and fitness and resolved to make decisive changes in her life. "Once you've read that, you really can't carry on being as lazy as you were and stuffing all that unhealthy junk inside you!" she told everyone who wanted to listen (or not). Michaela acquired a home gym and worked out vigorously for 45 minutes a day, not letting even the initial muscle pains stop her. She radically changed her diet, eating unrefined foods, fruit, vegetables, lots of protein and taking all kinds of vitamin and mineral supplements and deleting fats, white flour products and other "toxins" from the menu. She felt newborn! Then the first exceptions began to creep in: days on which she exercised for only 15 minutes a day, or not at all. Then she could only manage it twice a week; soon it was once a week. Eventually she suffered such pangs of conscience at the mere sight of the home gym that she put it in the basement. Her diet ran a similar course. Soon, it just took too long to cook brown rice—risotto was much quicker with white. Phoning for a pizza was much quicker than peeling vegetables and chopping them up for the wok. More and more frequently she ate junk food in her break at work, and even the vitamin and mineral supplements were only taken sporadically.

Frustrated, Michaela looked at Harry over her glass of wine: "Why is it so difficult to change your life? Why is it almost impossible to leave old habits behind and instead adopt new, more sensible or healthier patterns of behavior—and to stick to them?"

I have come across this and similar questions again and again in my seminars, and in my own life too! Whether it's the daily run, healthy eating, reading books instead of watching so much TV, keeping a regular diary or having more time for family and friends—it simply doesn't seem to be enough to tell ourselves how useful and pleasing a particular development would be in our lives. And unfortunately in most cases it's not enough to start something

The little exception to the diet...

new with great enthusiasm. Many people give up after a time, firmly "supported" by the comfort offered by their inner saboteur, who provides them with an imaginative range of excuses.

Most people do not pay enough attention to the *power of our habits*, or to put it better, the *resistance to change* of the same. This is an incredibly powerful force, but most of the time we don't notice it. As a consequence, we tend to underestimate this force mightily. And so, of course, we fall victim to it again and again. In order to handle this force differently, it's a good idea to examine the way it works within us.

When you start a new activity, it's often as if you were *swimming against the current*, against the current of your familiar habits.

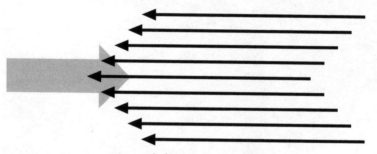

A new behaviour pattern at first means
swimming against the current

This *having to swim against the current* is extremely tiring. No wonder, then, that many people sooner or later throw in the towel and give up. It's understandable, but dooms the project. Exhausted as we are, our little saboteur has us back in its embrace.

That was the bad news! There is some good news too. This problem exists *only at the beginning* and in time it will turn into satisfaction, indeed into pleasure. Because, unlike a river that will never change direction, we can change the direction (that is, the "run of our programming") within our nervous system. We can, so to speak, reprogram ourselves and thereby change our habits.

However, a condition for such reprogramming is that we take the rules and qualities that govern our nervous systems into account. Nervous systems may seem stubborn, but they are in no way malicious. They are quite capable and willing to learn new things, you just have to know how to go about it.

Imagine that you are walking across a dewy meadow on a radiant summer morning. After a while, you turn and see the trail you have left in the wet grass. But the effect of this trail does not last for long. After only a short time, the grass will straighten up again, and you won't be able to see where you crossed the meadow. Only if you cross the meadow again and again along the same line will a track gradually develop, narrow at first, later maybe even becoming a wider path.

Reprogramming your nervous system works in much the same way. If you want to create a new "behavior track", you must repeat the new activity again and again, and always in the same place, that is to say, *in the same way* and best of all *at the same time*. For instance, run every day at the same time along the same route. After a certain time, once you have created a new track in your nervous system, that is, you have "implemented" a new habit, you will no longer be swimming against the current, but will have succeeded in changing its direction and you will now be swimming *with the current* of your new habits! In pictorial form, it looks like this:

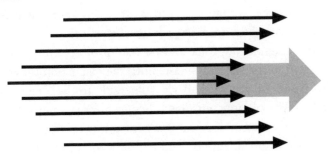

Take care. Beginnings are difficult times—from two points of view. For one thing, the investment required at the beginning is particularly high. You are, after all, swimming against the current of your old programming—which often needs a lot of strength. For another, the "return on investment" (the currently perceptible gain in units of feeling good) may at this stage seem relatively low. To take the example of running, pains in the feet, breathing problems and muscle ache may predominate at the beginning, before you realize how much you are benefiting your health. If you want to become a non-smoker, frustration due to lack of nicotine and having to do without the familiar actions—such as lighting a cigarette after a meal—will predominate, while the improvement in your shortness of breath may still scarcely be felt. If you continue steadily and stay with the task in hand, you'll soon reach the "magic point" where the relationship between investment and return switches over (you have now reached the point, so to speak, where you have created a new track and a new habit). From now on, your project will no longer cost you so much effort and strength, while the profit for your wellbeing and fitness continues to rise. Now you really do have a good return on investment! This "magic point" is, in a sense, the "point of no return". From now on it will become ever-more unlikely that you will turn back, as the profit is steadily rising and the amount of effort invested steadily decreasing. The graph on the next page shows this most impressively. Your saboteur now has a bad hand of cards if it wants to trick you out of this new behavior pattern. It may not even want to any more, as it is now swimming with the current in your new behavior!

As the diagram opposite shows, new projects are particularly endangered in the start-up phase, until the magic point is reached. In this phase we are particularly vulnerable to the attacks of our inner foe. The obvious mismatch between return and investment gives our saboteur a plethora of arguments as to why it would be better if we stopped, gave up and got back to our familiar comfort zone as fast as possible. You must overcome this "mountain" in the early phase. Because, in this "mountain range", we often have to reckon on the most cunning ambushes by our little saboteurs, we will call this point "Saboteur's Ridge".

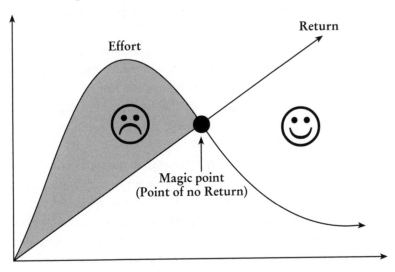

**In the "Saboteur's Ridge" phase, the return may be lower than the investment. Return on investment increases once we are past the point of no return.**

We still need to answer the question as to when you can be sure that you have overcome the Saboteur's Ridge phase and reached the magic point of no return. This is a very good question, and you are quite justified in asking it. It is very possible that you may from time to time (even after only a short period) have the feeling that your return is already higher than the investment of effort. Enjoy the feeling—but don't deceive yourself! Many of those who thought, too soon, that they were safe have been defeated by an unexpected saboteur's attack. In general, experts tell us, it takes four to six weeks before a new behavior pattern is firmly "fixed". These values are based on experience and may be of interest, but in the end you yourself and your personality are the only determining factors. It is quite possible that you will need much less time—or rather more.

Using the following simple test, you can (at least in most cases) find out whether you have reached the magic point or indeed have gone past it.

If you are forced to make an *exception* (for example, because you need to go to the airport at three in the morning and taking your morning run isn't possible), and you have the feeling that *you are missing something*, then you have probably passed the magic point. If on the contrary you almost feel *relief* that you don't have to run today, then you still have some way to go!

Whatever the behavior pattern or change in question, you are the one who has to find out how firmly you are in the saddle. But a saddle is not an armchair! The point of no return should not be understood as an insurance against attacks and ambushes by your inner saboteur. It will happen again and again that you will need to make a considerable effort and overcome your reluctance. After all, there is no return without investment, no feeling good without some effort. But it will be nowhere near as difficult to carry on as it was in the early stages.

## How to Get Over Saboteur's Ridge

Of course, even in the early stages of a long-term change in behavior the five ground rules that you have already come across in the "Strategic Equipment in Five Steps" chapter apply: the need for a definite decision, a clear plan of your goal, starting at once if possible, regular monitoring of success and celebrating of interim goals. In order not to give up and leave the field to the saboteurs, you also need to take the following tips into account:

- Make the start easy on yourself
- Use the power of rhythm
- Stay with the job, despite the occasional exception
- Use the "sandwich technique"

How these succeed is described below.

## *Make the start easy on yourself*

Because the start is the most difficult part, you should make it as easy as possible for yourself. One important rule is:

**Start in a small way—so you'll experience success sooner—and increase your workload bit by bit**

Develop a good feeling for the place where your *personal limits* lie, and don't do too much at the beginning. We can't stress often enough that *too great a challenge is the number one motivation killer* and therefore one of the main reasons why good intentions fail.

A friend of mine wanted to do something for his health and decided to go running. As his brother ran at least one hour a day, he started off at once with an ambitious 45 minutes and already by the next day—plagued by muscle ache—he had to take a break. He was grateful for the opportunity to stop, offered to him by his little foe. Running wasn't for him, surely this attempt proved it! However, his brother encouraged him to try again, but to start in a small way. So he started in the first week with 10 minutes a day, 15 in the second, increasing it slowly to 20, 25, 30 and more minutes. The decisive thing was never to exceed his personal "just about feeling good" limit. Today, he runs 50 minutes a day, and has now been doing so for two years. His little saboteur joins him on his runs.

A fit sportsperson will manage 100 press-ups in one go with no problems. If that's your goal too, you could start out sensibly with, for example, five press-ups a day, increasing them to ten after one week, then to 15 and so on. If you continue steadily, it will take only 20 weeks, that is, less than six months, to reach your desired level.

You want to allow yourself half an hour's quiet every day so that you don't get swallowed up by the stresses of daily life? Start with five or ten minutes a day—maybe on a day when you're not working and have more time for yourself anyway, or as part of a holiday. It could happen that your old programming, which hardly knew what a rest was, might prove to be very disruptive and, in the early stages, interrupt your "mini-meditation" with a lot of inner unrest and disturbing thoughts. Don't let that bother you. You will gradually notice how much more relaxed you are because of your new habit. For this very reason, you should not force yourself into a "meditation marathon" at the start. Your inner saboteur is just waiting for you to take on too much and will whisper in your ear that there are more urgent things to do than to withdraw like this.

Or is "read more, watch TV less" an item on your program? Initially, it's better to swap one TV evening per week for a reading evening instead of prohibiting TV altogether. And you don't have to read for three hours solid right at the beginning. If you read only ten pages a day, you will manage a 200-page book in 20 days. That will give you around 18 books a year—if you don't take any breaks from reading.

## Use the power of rhythm

One of the most important secrets for *firmly fixing* new behavior patterns in life is:

**Whatever you want to do long-term, do it if possible at the *same time*, in the *same place* and in the *same manner*!**

*Rhythmic repetition of the same action* has an amazing effect on our nervous systems. It is the key to reprogramming, for the "installation", so to speak, of new behavior patterns on your "hard drive". The importance of rhythmic repetition simply cannot be repeated often enough! Even that sentence should be repeated several times. So once again:

**To create new behavior patterns, you need constant, rhythmic repetition.**

That should do for now. We may come back to this point a few times, until your little saboteur can no longer bear to hear it and stops listening, takes no further notice and probably goes to sleep. This is the point: rhythmic repetition of the same thing puts your inner saboteur into a kind of trance, makes it sleepy and reduces its resistance more and more.

You've probably experienced it yourself in various situations in life. *The more often you repeat an action, the less your inner resistance to doing it becomes.* So use the power of rhythmic repetition to support you!

Especially in the early stages, take your run at the same time each day, for example, in the mornings at 6.30 or in the evenings at 5.30. The best thing initially is to choose the same route each time, which you can of course gradually extend. This is the way to create your "track across the meadow". In a short time, due to repro-gramming, your nervous system will, in a manner of speaking, "call" you for your run, as your inner clock switches to "run" at around 6.30am or (5.30pm). Once you are on your familiar route, your nervous system automatically knows what to do here—run, run and run …

If you have decided to meditate every day, then fix a *definite, constant* time for this project—a time at which you are unlikely to be disturbed. It's best to choose a fixed, constant place for meditating. Time and place will increasingly become "memory anchors" within your nervous system, and your inner program will switch to "meditation" at this time and in this place. Similarly, the prayer rugs used by Muslims function as "anchors" for prayer, which is of course always held at the same times (as in all religious traditions). Gradually, once daily meditation has become a matter of course for you, you will have no difficulties in switching off and listening within yourself almost at any time and in any place.

## *Stay with the job, despite exceptions.*

The *exceptions* described on page 75 provide the saboteurs with one of their best opportunities for tricking us thoroughly. They are only too happy to entice us to take some outside circumstance as the occasion to interrupt a new behavior pattern, until the exceptions mount up and we possibly give up altogether. Every exception interrupts the reprogramming process described above. This is why it is so important in the early stages (up to the "point of no return") to watch out for the dangerous exceptions and to stay with the job. To support yourself in this, you can use three main tried-and-tested methods:

**The exception test:** Not every exception we make has to be a saboteur's trap. There really are situations in which other matters are sensibly given priority. A business trip, for example, illness or someone who urgently needs our help could make an exception necessary. In the same way, the unexpected visit of a friend we have not seen for a long time can lead to us deliberately putting off our fitness program or our reserved meditation time for that day.

However, it's important to test ourselves within to see if we are using the special occasion merely as an *excuse* for an interruption or if the unexpected event really does have priority. In most cases we will recognize the truth at once. If not, use the *formula* below to check if your little saboteur is at all involved. Let's assume you want to make an exception to behavior pattern X because of a special event Y. Is your attitude one of "Actually, I really want to do X, but Y does definitely have priority right now", or do you rather feel relief, "Actually, I should do X now; how nice, I can make an exception because of Y"? If the latter is the case—hi there, your little saboteur says hello!

**The catch-up technique:** If you really were prevented from putting your new behavior pattern into practice, and also if your inner saboteur has managed to wring an exception out of you, then *catch up with what you've missed at the next opportunity*—best of all the next day, but within a week at the latest! However, you should be suspicious if catching-up occasions come more and more often. You're then in danger of the psychological mountain becoming so high that it will be easy for your saboteur to make you give up the whole thing as "far too much work" or tell you "you can't get through that any more". Therefore, if you find that too many catch-up dates have piled up, we recommend that you "clear the table" and start again—and this time, be more consistent.

**The five-minute trick:** It can of course happen from time to time that because of pressing external circumstances you realize that your normal program won't fit into the time you have available. Now you need to stay with the job and not let go. Even if you normally run for 25 minutes a day, allow yourself at least five minutes on days like this. For example, just put on your tracksuit and run once round the block. It won't advance your fitness program by much—which is just the excuse that your saboteur will give you. But that's not important here. The decisive point is that you don't permit a wholesale exception. You help your nervous system and yourself if you don't interrupt your reprogramming. Here, even a minimal program is better than nothing. Keep going—it's worth it!

## The sandwich technique

As we've seen, it's not easy to establish a new behavior pattern. You can make it easier by placing the new behavior, which hasn't been "fixed" in your nervous system yet, between two existing habits that you don't want to change. You can, in a manner of speaking, use the current of the existing habits to carry the new one along.

If you have resolved to do a series of keep-fit exercises in the morning, you can "embed" these between cleaning your teeth and taking a shower. If you have decided on regular relaxation exercises, you can fit these into the time between lunch and your afternoon tea break.

The five pages that you might have recently decided you want to read a day could perhaps fit into the time between coming home and your customary time for switching on the TV.

> The important thing is always to carry out the three activities—two well-established ones and the new one in between—in the same order and, if possible, not to let any other activities come between. For the latter, your little saboteur is bound to have plenty of ideas …

All the tricks and strategies described above will support you in getting across "Saboteur's Ridge" as easily and safely as possible in the difficult early phase, so that you need to spend less and less effort overcoming your reluctance. Consider: if you constantly have to overcome your reluctance, you must be doing something wrong. At any rate, this applies to something you having been doing for a longer period of time. It could then be that it's not the right thing *for you*. If, in the long term, the return does not exceed the investment, then leave it. In such a case, look for something else that will also do you good but feels easier. The decisive point is that your new behavior pattern should be making you feel better. Your little saboteur will share this opinion.

## The secret of change

- Do one thing at a time
- Start in a small way
- Increase slowly
- Stay with the job
- But don't do too much

# 10
## FURTHER HELP: ALLIES,
## COMMITMENTS, INVESTMENTS

Instead of wandering lonely as a cloud as you struggle with your inner saboteur, act on the saying "Two heads are better than one". Or make binding agreements with yourself and others. How does this work? Read on!

## LOOK FOR ALLIES

6.30am. The alarm went off. Sleepily, Julia dragged herself to the window. Oh no, it was raining! Running in this weather, after a mere six hours of sleep? No! Her little saboteur grunted, "Get back to bed, you'll catch something horrible!" She was almost back under the covers when she remembered with a shock that in ten minutes Esther and Michael would be waiting for her in the park. Yesterday evening, at the party, they agreed the time, as all three of them were struggling against their little saboteurs to go running. No, she wasn't about to show herself up like that. Quickly she pulled on her tracksuit trousers and trainers, while her little saboteur growled and snarled. "Be quiet and come with me. We won't run for long!" Soon, despite the wind and weather, three figures could be seen happily running through the park. Three? No, about 50 yards behind them three more figures were following, grunting and gasping. Later, as they had breakfast together, Julia, Esther and Michael admitted that none of them would ordinarily have gone running today—but none of them had dared to back out! The same happened over the following days. With the exception of real illness, or work-related obstacles, the three of them ran together every day—at least for the first three months. After that, they were so "addicted" to running that they often ran alone on occasion. Together, they started doing longer routes.—6.30am. The alarm went off. Sleet. The little saboteur was already outside; it had become addicted too.

*Agreements with others and joint action* provide some of the most powerful help in countering the (initial) objections made by your inner saboteur. In particular, they will protect you against those well-known *exceptions*. There are cases where I would give way if I were alone, but of course it is much more difficult to do so if I were to "lose face" in front of others. So:

**Arrange to go training together.** It doesn't matter whether you want to do running, cycling, rowing or general fitness training. The important thing is that the group should be *at a similar level of ability*. The slower people will feel the challenge is too great if they always have to struggle to keep up, and the faster ones will find the challenge too small and feel frustrated if they have to slow down all the time because of the others. You know, of course, that too great and too small a challenge are both number-one motivation killers.

**Also agree to join up for joint one-off actions.** It can be a lot of fun clearing out the basement or the attic together, to help each

other in the garden, build that shed together with a friend, or even arrange for a clearing-up day in the office (with music, of course, including catering and a party at the end of it).

**Make pacts with others.** The example below will show you what this could look like:

> I was 12 when that very important question came up: to smoke or not to smoke. I had tried a cigarette once but didn't get more than halfway down. It not only tasted awful, it made me feel really sick (with the obvious consequences ...). On the other hand, there was the relaxed and cool effect of taking a cigarette out of my pocket and lighting it in the presence of others—especially in the presence of admired representatives of the opposite sex. It is thanks to a pact with Wolfgang, my friend at the time, that I have never smoked more than that half cigarette. We exchanged opinions at length on this problem and were both divided between "Tastes horrible, it's bad for your health and costs money" on the one hand and "It's cool and casual and makes an impression" on the other. I don't know any more which of us had the idea, but we made an agreement not to smoke till our 18th birthdays. Whoever broke this pact would have to pay the other 100 marks. That was a lot of money for us in those days. But the vital thing for us wasn't the money, it was the pact! You can't break a pact made between friends. Apart from that, we soon made the discovery that, when asked why we didn't smoke (as we often were), the story of our pact impressed the girls a good deal. That, they thought, really was cool. A few years ago I met Wolfgang again at a 20th graduation anniversary reunion. He too hasn't smoked to this day!

Together we can crack it—the little saboteurs go running as well

It needn't always be such a "life or death" matter as smoking. *Pacts* or *agreements* with others can support you in all sorts of circumstances:

- To complete a certain matter by a certain date
- To go through a joint weight loss program together or
- To do someone a favor or give them some pleasure every day

Some time ago, a strange, large-scale joint action was reported in the papers. In the USA, a whole town had decided to lose weight. As part of the "76 tons of fun" action, the citizens of Philadelphia had agreed to lose 76 tons of weight between them. The Philadelphia 76ers basketball team supported the action, and even the mayor joined in. (Source: the editorial of the magazine *Fit for Fun*, June 2001.)

A remarkable campaign indeed! Whether we should copy it is a matter of opinion. It can be very motivating if thousands of people do something together. But a personal pact with a friend or even a coach can motivate just as much.

**Go to places where there are people with the same idea.** If *several people are working towards the same goal*, that is incredibly motivating. Many students have already discovered how working in a library, where others too are sitting silently with their books, can increase their own discipline and motivation. And for many people it's easier to sweat together in a gym than at home on their own fitness equipment, especially if they make use of the group programs offered at the gym. For difficult projects, there are even *clubs* of people with the same goal. The success of "Weightwatchers" or "Alcoholics Anonymous" is to an extent due to acting as a kind of association of people with the same problem who are supporting one another.

**Avoid people with negative attitudes.** Keep well away from skeptics, the frustrated, pessimists, cynics, grumblers and other doom-mongers who have not only given up themselves but want to keep others from turning their lives around. Unfortunately, their envy of the successful is widespread, and many people who have given their own inner saboteur free rein are not in favor of others taming theirs.

**Don't compare yourself with those who are supposed to be better.** Comparisons with others who appear to get things organized more easily, more quickly or better are very discouraging. The little saboteur growths in strength when comparisons are made (as we have shown on page 161).

## SECURE PROJECTS BY MAKING COMMITMENTS

Don't just make a *binding agreement with yourself*—enter into a *commitment with others*. These can be friends, family, your company, even the public at large. A publicly announced project is not so easy to give up! It can sometimes even be helpful to have a friend or your coach phone you at agreed intervals, or call personally, to ask how things are going; or commit yourself to making a report once a week, for example, even if this is only a postcard ("Everything OK—I'm getting there!"). The effect of *regular monitoring* is also one of Weightwatchers' success factors.

## GET THAT RETURN ON INVESTMENT

When I met a former colleague from my team again a short while ago, I almost didn't recognize her. This once plump and rather phlegmatic person had become a slender, athletic woman. Beaming, she said she had done all this in only 18 months in the gym. Amazed, I asked for details, as I remembered that she had often said previously that gyms were definitely not for her. In fact, her little saboteur had started to snarl at the very thought of such places, and its range of excuses was almost invincible. But then she simply joined the best and most expensive gym in the area and signed a contract for two years. Now there was no going back. As she was by nature a thrifty person, it was a success. She had to get the benefit of these 90 euros per month. Success was plain to see—and even her little saboteur had lost a considerable amount of weight.

Many people find it hard to make no use of a financial investment. Would you leave your expensive trainers, new bicycle or exercise equipment standing in the corner unused? The purchase of a top-quality computer or musical instrument can exert a "pull" to get cracking and learn how to use it. If not, the money would be wasted. That may not be the ideal and sole motivating factor, but for some people it can supply the additional push. Why shouldn't you make use of this factor? Buying equipment or joining the gym is in any case the first step! Keep going, and you will indeed get a good return on your investment.

# 11
## NEGOTIATING WITH YOUR
## LITTLE SABOTEUR

In especially difficult cases of sabotage, where you have been struggling for a long time with your inner slacker, it could be a good idea to *negotiate* with your little foe. This may seem surprising at first. You will of course ask yourself *how* you talk to or even negotiate with your inner opponent. However, in psychological practice today it has often been shown that those who openly and honestly seek to contact their subconscious will find a way. And the same applies to contacting your inner saboteur.

Let us assume (as one of the fundamental principles of psychology has it) that there is a positive intent behind every form of behavior, even if this may seem quite absurd at first glance. "Positive" here refers only to you alone, not necessarily to others. It could also be that your inner saboteur is using its campaigns for some positive purpose on behalf of you personally. You should therefore ask it what positive intention its objections might possibly have. Ask it what it has maybe been trying to tell you in a roundabout way for some time—without you having heard it (or wanting to hear it)! What good purpose could, in certain circumstances, be served by the behavior pattern that you are desperately struggling to change? The object is to find out the purposes of your inner saboteur if it constantly makes you do one thing when you want to do another.

Let us assume that a fairly disciplined and hard-working young man has been struggling for years (with no success) against the obsessive need that makes him watch TV for one or two hours after lunch, before he can continue working. As he works from home as a freelance journalist, his working conditions "permit" such apparently "crazy" behavior (to compensate, he often works in the evenings till 10 or 11pm). Could there be a positive intent behind such behavior? Yes, the little saboteur cries, otherwise its owner would work with no breaks at all. The purpose of the TV sabotage is to keep him away from work for at least one or two hours a day!

The next stage of negotiations is for you to ask your saboteur if it would be prepared not to sabotage you any more if you were to fulfil this purpose in *some other way*. Let us assume that you have, as part of your personality, a *creative adviser* within yourself: ask it to advise you as to other ways in which you can achieve this positive purpose, and in such a way as to gain your other goals as well. Go "inside yourself" until you have come up with three possible options.

> The journalist mentioned above could, for example, consider one of the following instead of the meaningless TV-watching: first, to go for a walk every day for an hour; second, to go and have a sauna three times a week; or third, to meditate for half an hour a day and then spend another 30 minutes in his home gym.

Offer the three solutions to your inner saboteur and ask it if it agrees to one of these or if it needs something more to see its positive intention realized.

Then seal your negotiations with a *contract with your inner saboteur*. In this contract, you agree that you really will put the chosen option into practice, and your saboteur, for its part, agrees not to hinder you any more in this matter. And you know, of course, that contracts are binding! If you don't keep to your obligations, your little saboteur will torpedo you utterly.

Many people have been able to release numerous "saboteur blockades" using this method. You can only find out whether it will help you by daring to make the attempt!

Have fun, and we wish you success in your negotiations!

| Negotiations with your little saboteur | |
|---|---|
| Initial situation: | You want to do X.<br>Your saboteur makes you do Y. |
| Fundamental assumption: | There is a positive intent behind every form of behavior. |
| Step 1: | Ask your saboteur what positive intent it has for you in making you do Y. |
| Step 2: | Honor this positive intent! |
| Step 3: | Ask your saboteur if it will stop Y if you can fulfil the purpose of Y by some other means. |
| Step 4: | Together with the "creative adviser" within you, look for three other options to achieve the purpose of Y by other means. |
| Step 5: | Offer these three options to your saboteur and have it choose the best one. Ask it if that is enough. |
| Step 6: | Put the seal on everything with a contract. |
| Step 7: | Keep to the contract. |

# 12
## Saboteur Training and
## a Saboteur Diary

"No, I daren't!" seven-year-old Natalie cried, looking down from the 10-foot-high diving board to the pool below. Not two minutes before, she had told her father that she wanted to dive today as well, and for the first time she climbed with him up to the high board. From up here, it all looked very different. Natalie was torn between her desire to do the high dive at last, and her fear. "OK", her father said, "that's quite normal, I was scared the first time too. But who is it who actually daren't, you or your little saboteur?" Natalie, who was already well acquainted with her tricky little companion, smiled: "My little saboteur, of course!" "Then hold it by the hand, give it lots of encouragement and dive together with it. It might dare to jump then." Natalie stretched out her hand, murmured a few calming words and then—splash—she had dived into the water. When she came up again, she was beaming—and her little saboteur probably was too.

Take your little saboteur by the hand

Back home, there was a saying that one should simply take the "ghost of fear" by the hand and do whatever one was afraid of. In this way, the fear would gradually disappear. This really is true:

**The best way of overcoming fear is *to do the thing one is afraid of.***

In a way, this applies not only to our handling of apprehension and fear but to anything where we find it difficult to overcome our reluctance; that is, everywhere we meet our little saboteur. You will tame your inner saboteur more quickly the more you train with it, the more often you go to meet it and dive with it into the "waters of challenge". *Saboteur training* means repeatedly doing larger or smaller *saboteur exercises*.

**As a saboteur exercise, do things *that challenge you, that you are nervous about doing or that are linked to a certain amount of risk.***

Try out new things, and dare to do crazy things as well. Keep searching for your personal "high diving boards"—and then, like little Natalie, take your companion by the hand and dive. Every dive will make your little saboteur a bit tamer and more trusting.

Do at least one *small* saboteur exercise *every day* and one *large* one *every year*. You may even soon find that this training is fun (as may your charming little saboteur). In a short time you will set up the *positive saboteur cycle* that you can see below. You come across a challenge, you confront it, you are successful, the resistance of your inner saboteur is reduced a bit and this means that your willingness to meet the next challenge is increased.

There is also, of course, the *negative saboteur cycle*. If you avoid the challenge, you experience failure, the resistance of your saboteur is increased and your willingness to meet the next challenge is reduced (as in the diversion procedure on page 70).

## The positive saboteur cycle

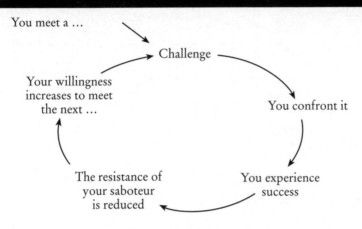

Don' t forget one thing:

**The decisive step is that you *meet the challenge*,
not necessarily the success!**

If you need to overcome your reluctance to talk to a stranger at a dance, the decisive point (as far as saboteur training is concerned) is that you *did* it, not *whether* you got a positive result (in the case of the high diving board, success occurs at the same time as you dive).

In order to have any success at all, it's important that you don't set your sights too high, that you look for challenges that you are able to take on.

Keep looking out for new, exciting, manageable exercises, and enter your training into a *saboteur diary*. There is an example on page 194.

Write down in this little book what you have done, what fears or doubts you had, what *exactly* was the nature of the challenge for you, whether you were successful or not, what feelings the result brought about in you and how your saboteur reacted. How did it

## Saboteur diary

Challenge

_____

_____

_____

What does my little saboteur say? (How)
Has it tried to trick me?

_____

_____

_____

(How) Have I overcome it?

_____

_____

_____

How did I feel afterwards? What have I learned?

_____

_____

_____

When shall I do it again?

_____

_____

_____

try and stop you? Did you avoid the challenge—was it too great for you? Do you want to try again? When? This diary must not and will not be just a diary of successes. That's not the point! The point is the training. In this way you will get to know yourself and your little companion better and better and gradually you will find your inner saboteur easier to deal with.

## A "Small" Saboteur Exercise Every Day

Each day offers many opportunities to do something unusual, challenging, crazy or extraordinary. At the end of the first day in my seminars, I often have the students perform some small saboteur exercise before the next morning (see also page 20). I'm always amazed at the imaginative opportunities for training with this little companion. Here is a small selection:

**Smile at strangers in public, greet them or even talk to them.** Why not just simply compliment someone who looks your type, invite them for a cup of coffee or ask if you can arrange to meet? "You can't do that!" "What will he/she think of me?" "They'll tell you to get lost!" "Don't do anything so embarrassing!" your little companion will cry. Of course, for most people the fear of rejection is very strong, so they don't even dare to try to contact others. Many spontaneous contacts that could enrich our lives collapse because we fear rejection. This is therefore an ideal training area for us and for our saboteurs. In most cases, you will find that the other person smiles back at you, returns your greeting or even, pleasantly surprised, accepts your invitation. Unless your attempt to make contact comes out as a clumsy pick-up line, the result is usually much better than your inner saboteur expects. And don't forget:

the reaction isn't important, only that you have stepped outside your limits.

Do something unusual or even crazy. This somewhat larger step could look like this:

- Speak to someone in the street and ask them how they like your tie or dress.
- Call the name of the stop out loud on the streetcar, bus or subway.
- Wear odd-colored socks or shoes.
- Have something put in a doggie bag at a restaurant (embarrassing—which makes it a good exercise).
- Try to bargain about the price of something in a shop (this is less unusual now than it used to be, but if *you* have to overcome your reluctance, then it's still a good exercise for you).

**Experiment with your habits and do something different from usual.** Here, too, there are numerous options:

- Go to work by some other means: ride a bike, use public transport or even run to work (if you can shower and change there).
- Instead of talking, spend a whole day practising listening and paying attention to others. This can work wonders.
- Leave out something that has become a habit: drink your coffee or tea unsweetened for a week, or don't smoke for a whole day.
- Do something quite different at lunchtime: go to a park or a café that you don't know, take a walk or relax in some other way by listening to music, instead of going to the canteen or the same restaurant again.
- Make small journeys of discovery: go to a place where you have never been, whether this is a part of town you rarely go to, or a shop in which you have never been (recommended by Spencer Johnson in his book *One Minute for Myself*). These small adventures will break up your routine for you.

**Do something that you have been putting off.** This may involve writing a letter that is long overdue, making a supposedly (or actually) difficult phone call, or initiating a problematic discussion in the family or at work.

**Do something unexpected and nice for someone.** Little things can mean so much. We're often simply too lazy to take this little step. So even a "small" good deed counts as a saboteur exercise:

- How about giving someone flowers for a change? If you aren't the sort of person who always gives flowers, the effect could amaze you. Whether it's your partner in life, your colleagues at work or friends—the more unexpected, the greater the effect. Just do it. A single flower is enough! You don't need to turn up with a dozen roses right away. Even giving someone you meet in the street a single flower is a good exercise to carry out with your little companion. An interesting variation is recommended by Matt Weinstein in his book *Managing to Have Fun*: lend a bunch of flowers, to a colleague at work for example, with instructions to pass it on to someone else after an hour—then other people can enjoy it too. Your little saboteur will resist a bit, but only at first, and then it will have fun too.
- It can be simpler, but no less effective, to send someone a postcard. And if your inner companion wants to object that you've got no time or you won't be able to think of anything clever or witty in a hurry, then just write, "Thinking of you! Love from Seema."
- And what about a few units of comfort? Praise your friends and colleagues, give them recognition and compliment them a little (don't let it become a habit—then it won't count as a training exercise, of course!).

**Say thank you.** This is something else that many people tend to forget, or don't pull themselves together to do it, or have their little saboteurs put off until it is too late. Whether it's a recommendation at work, some practical help or just something we might take as "a matter of course", there are always opportunities to say thank you.

A friend of mine was an absolute "professional" in this department. He even thanked plumbers or taxi drivers if they came on time—it's not every one that does! It's said that Hillary Clinton spends up to two hours a day thanking people who have supported her in some way. Her little saboteur certainly isn't offering any more resistance in this matter.

**Learn to accept things from others.** There are not a few people who find it difficult to accept a gift or a favor if they don't have the immediate opportunity to do something in return. This is also a good area for training. If your inner saboteur grumbles too much, you'll find help in the book by Matt Weinstein mentioned on the previous page. Accept the gift or the favor as a "loan" and promise (if necessary promise yourself) that you will do something similar for somebody else as soon as the opportunity arises. Your "something in return" then doesn't need to be done for the person who did the original favor.

A short time ago I wanted to give a friend a book, but he objected, saying he couldn't accept it just like that, with no special reason. So I said "OK, if you don't like the book, send it back to me, but if you think it's good, buy another copy and give it to somebody who'll enjoy receiving it." Immediately, his little saboteur shut up, took the book and began to read it.

**Create a bit of order.** It doesn't matter where. Clear out a drawer, your car or some area where things have collected. It's not necessary to do it for yourself. You could clean up the tea room at work "just for fun" or pick up a cigarette packet lying in the street and throw it in the nearest litter bin. You little companion might object, "But *you* didn't drop it!" True, but afterwards, the street looks cleaner, and you've created a bit of order—not just for others, you did it for yourself as well. Every bit of *external* tidying up has an effect upon our *internal* mood. Afterwards, you too could be giving a "tidy" impression.

**"Switch off" your saboteur through meditation every day.** One of the quickest ways of regenerating ourselves and getting back in touch with our sources of inner strength is to switch off and sink into ourselves, into inner silence. It would of course be useful if you were familiar with a meditation technique such as yoga or autogenic training. However, to learn such techniques from scratch might mean a serious struggle with your inner saboteur. It will be enough, therefore, if you just sit quietly for five minutes once or twice a day, best of all with eyes closed, and calmly pay attention to your breathing. You don't need the "lotus position" or any particular technique. A park bench would be suitable, the chair at your desk, if you can relax for five or ten minutes at your workplace, or your seat in the train or aircraft. When you start "switching off", it might happen that your saboteur confronts you with the best tricks in its range of excuses: "No time for that now!" "You can do it later!" "You can't just sit and do nothing" and so on. Try it anyway, as a small saboteur exercise. It will soon come to appreciate the good points of meditation and join you!

We could carry on listing possible exercises for a long time. There are no limits to your imagination. However, the point is not to make an exhaustive list of exercises—the important thing is that you find the training opportunities that are possible for you. A suitable opportunity is anything:

- where you step out of your everyday routine for a short time
- where you overcome some reluctance
- that you always wanted to do anyway.

The only important thing, as mentioned before, is that you don't take on too great a challenge and that it is fun. Then your little saboteur will find it fun too.

So that this project doesn't just remain in the world of good intentions (if you want to go in for training!), you should now take up paper and pen and note down ten possibilities or ideas that spontaneously come into your mind as possible saboteur exercises. The examples above could serve as inspiration.

And when do you want to start with your exercise (the vital word is "deadline")? Watch out, your little companion is at the ready. Good luck!

## One Large Saboteur Training Project a Year (at Least)

Once a year (or indeed several times) you could take up a project that presents a greater challenge, or one of longer duration:

**Take on a large-scale clear-out.** You could spend a week (or spread it out over a longer period of time) thoroughly clearing out your "external life". Throw out all the useless things that you carry around with you as ballast: in the basement, the attic, the garage, your wardrobes, all those piles that you were going to look through "sometime", all those books that you will probably never read and that just gather dust on the shelves ... All this doesn't just block up your space, but also your *energy*. It's amazing how much energy is released in the lives of people who clear out their lives from top to bottom. Karen Kingston's book *Clear Your Clutter with Feng Shui* provides good inspiration and plenty of help. It's quite possible that your saboteur will come up in advance with lots of objections and

**You can meditate together with your little saboteur**

201

an imaginative mix of excuses. But once you've started, you find out how liberating and satisfying it is, and your saboteur will feel the same. Reports say that little saboteurs have in many cases even been spotted helping out …

**"Clear out" your body.** The inside should match the outside. Clearing out the cellar and the attic isn't the only thing that feels good. *Clearing out* and *detoxing* your body once a year will increase health and wellbeing. To do without certain indulgences for a period of time (during Lent, for instance) is good saboteur training. As the person concerned, you will know best whether the indulgence involved is alcohol, nicotine, coffee or meat. Taking part in a one- or two-week detox or health fast at a health farm is also a suitable exercise. The challenge here is not so great either: if everyone around you is doing the same thing, your companion will soon join in voluntarily. Some of my seminar students prefer mental to physical "detox" and do without TV for a month. It's exciting to see what a TV-free period can do. Test it!

**Meet sports challenges.** Anything to do with *sport* is an excellent subject for larger-scale saboteur training. Whether you take part in a special daily training program for a month at a gym, prepare for a marathon or even dare to attempt a parachute or bungee jump—as long as you don't risk physical damage, these would be good opportunities to tame your inner opponent.

**Withdraw from everyday life for a while.** For some people, it can be a healthy spiritual challenge to take part in a *retreat*. Whether you do meditation exercises, take part in a meditation seminar or just stay alone at a monastery for one or two weeks, such a step often requires that you overcome considerable reluctance, but the inner riches you can gain are great. At the end of the time, your little saboteur will usually be quite quiet and will smile peacefully as it meditates alongside you.

**Break through your everyday routine with an adventure holiday.** Your little saboteur will firmly advise against trekking in the Himalayas or a desert safari, but if you take part in such a project, it will come along too and be a little more tamed when it returns home. In the same way, you can test what it's like to hike for three days or a week alone somewhere or to go on a holiday quite different from your usual vacation trips, perhaps returning to a backpack and tent once more if you have been staying in multiple starred hotels for years. Or travel far on land or sea by bike, by tramp steamer or in a motor caravan. You little friend will come too.

**Take part in personal development seminars.** If, apart from saboteur training, you have definite goals for personal development, taking part in an appropriate *seminar* can be challenging and enriching. There are plenty on offer. Choose carefully which topics could assist you in your personal situation.

The above are a few suggestions for larger-scale saboteur training. There are certain to be numerous other options. If you can't think of any more, you need only ask your new friend. It will never be so tame that there are no more challenges for training with it.

# 13

## A Summary:
## The 50 Best Tips for
## Dealing with your
## Little Saboteur

You now have detailed information on how to make friends with your little saboteur, how to live in peace with it and still put your plans into action. Here again are the 50 most important tips in summary form. The page number at the end of each tip indicates the corresponding passage in the book and will make it easier for you to recap on the information that is most important to you. For each particular problem, you can look up the appropriate way to solve it at any time.

**1. Recognizing where you meet the little saboteur**
Become aware in which areas in life your inner slacker is most likely to obstruct and sabotage you (filling out the checklist will be a help).                                                *Page 22 ff.*

**2. Recognizing the ways in which it tricks you**
Identify the tricks and tactics most often used by your saboteur (checklist and hit list will help).             *Page 90 ff.*

### 3. Accept your little saboteur

You can't run away from it, you can't drive it away and you can't lock it up for long. You can only learn to tame it and accept and integrate it as a (necessary and sensible) part of your personality. *Page 97 ff.*

### 4. Discover its positive intentions for you

Assuming that your little saboteur (though you may only have experienced it as an opponent before now) has positive intentions for you in your life, what could these be? *Page 109 ff.*

### 5. Sometimes you should listen to your little saboteur

Resistance from your little saboteur is not always damaging. Sometimes it wants to protect you from doing too much, and make you aware of sensible limits in your life. You can learn from it to take care of yourself. *Page 102 ff.*

### 6. Learn from your little saboteur

You can learn from it—how to be a child again from time to time, that is, how to live for the moment, in the present, to take care of your pleasure in the moment, to release your inner clown and joker, to be spontaneous, to do something crazy once in a while, to cry or laugh and to rediscover your other childlike potential. *Page 108 ff.*

### 7. Quickly learn to decipher the saboteur's code

"Translate" the saboteur's excuses, those which it uses to make you lie to yourself, into their real meanings. This will make you conscious of the saboteur's real motives, and you will gain the freedom to make your own decisions and to take responsibility. *Page 111 ff.*

### 8. Choose "labels of opportunity"

Choice of words influences your view of things and your feelings. So take care which words you choose! In future, instead of "I have to", "I ought to", "I should", say "I want to", "I'd like to", "I can", "I will" or "I have the opportunity to". This will not change the facts, but will change the frame of mind in which you approach matters. *Page 113 ff.*

### 9. Focus on solutions

Instead of describing a situation as "insoluble", think how you could find a solution. For example, ask "How can I best manage that?" instead of "I can't do that!"; "How can I go on?" instead of "I'm stuck!" *Page 117 ff.*

### 10. View "negative" points as preliminary stages for future success

See problems as chances, difficulties as challenges, mistakes as aids in orientating yourself and failures as interim stages on the way to success. *Page 117 ff.*

### 11. Don't put yourself under too much pressure

Put yourself under pressure all the time and you won't have much fun in life. You'll also arouse the counter-pressure from your inner saboteur. The greater the pressure, the more aggressive your little saboteur will be. *Page 121 ff.*

### 12. Mount a pincer campaign against your little saboteur

Imagine, on the one hand, the gain the behavior pattern you are striving for will bring. On the other hand, clearly visualize the disadvantages that will occur if you give up your plans.

*Page 123 ff.*

### 13. Seek out challenges

One of the definitive factors in having fun doing anything is challenge—but only if the challenge is in balance with your own capabilities. "Flow" and happiness are often to be found at the limits of challenge. *Page 126 ff.*

### 14. Avoid too great a challenge

Too small a challenge and, in particular, too great a challenge are the biggest motivation killers in life. If you constantly overstretch yourself and no longer listen to the warnings of your little saboteur, you will suffer all the more from its acts of sabotage. *Page 127 ff.*

### 15. Make definite decisions

A clear decision is a pre-condition for the success of your plans. Make a list of all the projects you want to attack at long last, and then make a conscious decision for each point whether you will really start putting it into practice. If necessary, make a list of advantages and disadvantages.
*Page 134 ff.*

### 16. Follow the RKW and H principle

Get the necessary information, so that you REALLY KNOW WHY you want something, and acquire the necessary knowledge of HOW you can tackle the matter in the easiest and most effective way. *Page 139 ff.*

### 17. Experience the feeling of "performability"

If you want to achieve your goal, the goal must be not only objectively realistic, but you must in advance have the feeling that it can be done, the feeling that you can make it, that you really can put this plan into practice. *Page 141 ff.*

### 18. Use the technique of "eating oysters"

For small plans that you keep putting off, tackle them like eating oysters: one after the other, never two at once.

*Page 143 ff.*

### 19. Use the technique of "eating an elephant"

With larger projects, tackle them as you would eat an elephant: cut into small pieces (that is, divided into small, clear, time-limited units), bit by bit (that is, in small stages, step by step). If in doubt, it is better at the beginning to take undersized rather than oversized bites. *Page 143 ff.*

### 20. Word your goals positively

Negatively worded goals are not "brain-friendly"! Our brains can't "not think of" something. Not until you think of something you want to do instead can your brain picture the goal.

*Page 145 ff.*

### 21. Set exact, measurable goals

You can't put commands in the comparative into action. Without an exact task, your brain can't put your intentions into practice. You also can't check what you can't measure. So, instead of "get up earlier", say exactly "get up every day at 6 o'clock". *Page 147 ff.*

### 22. Set dates in writing

Dates in writing are essential for putting your projects into practice. Without deadlines, your little saboteur is in charge. Set fixed end deadlines, interim dates and fixed individual deadlines for each day—and enter these into a time schedule.

*Page 148 ff.*

### 23. Plan in spare time and buffer zones

Reserve at least one-third more time than you initially think necessary for putting your project into practice. Most people underestimate how long things will take. If you do happen to finish earlier, all the better! *Page 150 ff.*

### 24. Plan in breaks and leisure time

If you don't take enough breaks and allow yourself enough leisure time to regenerate, you'll soon be working at half strength and you'll need to deal with your little saboteur. But you need to plan breaks and leisure time too! *Page 151 ff.*

### 25. Give difficult projects Priority Number One

Projects where you expect to have a lot of opposition from your little saboteur, and for which you must make a great effort, should be given Priority Number One at the planning stage. Carry out such tasks as early as possible in the day. Saboteur business has priority! *Page 152 ff.*

### 26. Create presence

Make saboteur affairs into affairs of the heart; give them presence in your life. Remind yourself of them as often as possible during the course of the day: use notes, signs, notices, posters etc. *Page 153 ff.*

### 27. Create a brightly-lit goal

Picture to yourself in detail how things will look when you have reached your goal. The brighter the image of your goal, the weaker the resistance of your little saboteur! For your saboteur, images are more convincing than rational argument. Follow WYSIWYG: What You See Is What You Get! *Page 154 ff.*

### 28. "Shoot" an inner film

Use the mental techniques employed by professional sports people: create an inner film of how you will achieve your goal. The more detailed your inner film, the easier and quicker it will be to put it into practice. *Page 156 ff.*

### 29. Start at once

Take the first step as soon as possible. Just make a start and get ahead of your little saboteur. Just do it! Even if you're not quite in the mood. *Page 157 ff.*

### 30. Never give up because of a temporary bad mood

Don't throw in the towel in advance! Set stage deadlines as possible "revision dates" on which you can decide whether you really want to give up your resolution. Make a rational decision, not one based on a passing mood. *Page 160 ff.*

### 31. Put up with negative emotions

You should learn to put up with the occasional negative emotion instead of running away from these immediately. If the pull towards avoidance and giving way becomes too strong, then ask yourself if this matter really is essential, right now and immediately! *Page 160 ff.*

### 32. Move down a gear

If something becomes too strenuous for you, slow down your speed and reduce your workload. If nothing seems to go right any more, then throw in the towel—but for this one day only. Then you carry on! *Page 161 ff.*

### 33. Don't compare yourself with others

Don't compare yourself with those who are much better (that will pull you down) or with those who are much worse and give up or drop out (that will pull you out). If you can't avoid comparisons, then compare yourself with those who keep going (that will pull you along). *Page 161 ff.*

### 34. Monitor interim results

Monitoring will help with orientation (how far you have come and what still has to be done), with the adjustment of the plan (if this is necessary), and with motivation (by making yourself aware of your partial successes to date). Visualize your progress, write it down, draw it or paint it—and best of all, display the result somewhere where you can see it. *Page 161 ff.*

### 35. Don't forget the rewards

Plan in rewards right from the start and don't miss out on celebrating when you reach your goal (or the goal for this stage). Don't cheat yourself (or your little saboteur) out of the promised bonus. *Page 163 ff.*

### 36. Make the start as easy as possible

Your investment is greatest at the beginning, but the return may still be small. So make things as easy as possible at the start. Start in a small way. Don't overdo it. That will give you the quickest successful results. *Page 173 ff.*

### 37. Increase your effort slowly

Keep on moving the bar a little bit higher—slowly but steadily. Increase your tasks every week, for example, but take care and mind your limits. Or your little saboteur will bite!

*Page 173 ff.*

211

## 38. Use rhythmic repetition

In order to create a new habit, rhythmic repetition is needed. Whatever activity you want to "implement" for the long term, do it as far as possible at the same time, in the same place and in the same manner. You will also notice that the more frequently you repeat something, the weaker your saboteur becomes.

*Page 174 ff.*

## 39. Don't fall into the exceptions trap

Exceptions—particularly if they happen with increasing frequency—quickly lead to your giving up a project or a new behavior pattern. So test whether the exception really is necessary or whether it is only an excuse (which your little saboteur welcomes) not to make the effort. *Page 176 ff.*

## 40. Use the catch-up technique

If you are on occasion forced to make an exception, catch up with what you have missed at the first opportunity. On the same day if possible, within the next week at the latest. Don't let the catching-up appointments pile up! *Page 177 ff.*

## 41. Use the five-minute trick

If (especially in the early stages) you can't carry out your normal program due to time pressures, then stay with the job with a minimum program—even if it's only five minutes running a day. That will prevent you from losing your rhythm.

*Page 177 ff.*

## 42. Use the sandwich technique

Fix new behavior between two existing habits (which you don't want to change). The "current" of existing behavior will support your new behavior pattern and pull it along.

*Page 178 ff.*

## 43. Look for allies

Agree to meet up with others for training—it will protect especially against exceptions. Who is going to show themselves up by dropping out? Look for a group where all are at a similar level. *Page 180 ff.*

## 44. Make alliances and pacts

Make a pact with someone else about what you want and don't want to do—with sanctions for breaking the agreement if possible. It's best to fix your goals in writing. That makes them binding. *Page 181 ff.*

## 45. Look for places and for clubs where others are doing the same thing

Places where several people are doing the same as you will motivate and support you to join in. And you're unlikely to find exceptions in such places. *Page 184 ff.*

## 46. Avoid people with negative attitudes

Especially in the early stages, avoid skeptics, the frustrated, pessimists, cynics, grumblers and other doom-mongers. Such people have often resigned themselves to failing and then want to stop others from turning their lives around or improving them. *Page 184 ff.*

## 47. Secure your goals with commitments

Make binding arrangements with yourself, but also commit yourself in declarations to others. It's not so easy to give up on a publicly-declared intention! *Page 185 ff.*

## 48. Use the power of investment

You're less likely to waste financial investments. Whether it's a purchase or a subscription, you won't want to waste the money! The same should apply to invested effort. Your investment will encourage the return on investment.

*Page 185 ff.*

## 49. Negotiate with your little saboteur

Ask your little slacker what possible positive intentions might lie behind a particular act of sabotage. Honor this intention and look for other ways of putting your plan into practice. Make a contract with your little saboteur—a contract to be kept by both parties.

*Page 187 ff.*

## 50. Train regularly with your little saboteur

Do smaller saboteur exercises—something where you need to overcome some reluctance—every day. It's best to do one larger, more difficult project once a year (at least). In this way, you'll get to know yourself and your little companion better, and will tame it more and more.

*Page 190 ff.*

# 14
## CONCLUSION

We obviously all have a part of our personality that is always in our way, which sabotages our plans, and which we repeatedly have to struggle to overcome. We have referred to this part of our personality as "the little saboteur". However, there is a reason for its existence, and in many cases it pursues positive intentions on our behalf, intentions which we need to discover.

The inner saboteur can be tamed and turned from foe into friend. To do so, it is necessary to accept it, learn to listen to it, give it the niche in our lives to which it is entitled and at the same time to set limits for it.

In dealing with our inner companion, we can experience that the important thing in life is to keep on meeting challenges, without overstretching ourselves. It's rare that we can make decisive changes in our lives by brute force; we need to approach them slowly, carefully, in small steps and stages. Then our little slacker won't sabotage us.

With each person, the inner saboteur expresses itself differently, and it probably fulfils a different function for each person. So each one of us must learn in his or her way to live with the little saboteur, to find a way to tame it and make friends with it. But this way can be exciting, liberating and extremely enriching. Try it!

# AND WHAT HAPPENED AFTERWARDS ...

At the special conference of little saboteurs held to discuss this book, the proceedings were exceedingly exciting and unruly. By comparison, the annual conference had been almost quiet and peaceful. All the little saboteurs present had received a copy of the manuscript and read it, but the reactions varied greatly. The League of Saboteurs was divided.

The conservative faction was distrustful of the whole affair and the possible effect of the book. They held the whole thing to be a trick thought up by humans in their battle against the inner saboteur, with the end goal of final conquest and imprisonment. The conservatives demanded that a saboteurs' regeneration center be set up, with the aim of arousing new strengths in the "old" saboteurs and trying out new battle tactics. In particular, they planned a concentrated campaign of counter-measures to prevent the distribution of the book, the reading of it or at the very least any action on the advice contained in it. But nothing much came of these campaigns! They hadn't counted on their own inner saboteurs (some may not even have known they existed). At any rate, several representatives of the conservative faction couldn't even win the struggle to come to a decision (there's no point in it anyway ...); others claimed that one could try and do something; still others had decided, but never found the right time or were never in the right *mood to put their plans into practice; and the rest quickly broke off their campaigns when they saw that others weren't doing anything either...*

*The saboteurs in the liberal faction, on the other hand, welcomed the appearance of this book. They believed that someone had finally understood them. Much of the advice was after their own hearts, and they hoped for an end to old hostilities and a new era of cooperation and friendship.*

What about your little saboteur? Which faction does it belong to? In the end, it depends on you! You may need to take the first step and hold out your hand. If you can succeed in taming it and making it your ally, you can considerably improve your life. Then you won't need to fight a saboteur all the time any more, but you'll be putting your plans into practice together with a new friend.

And in this project, I wish you plenty of skill, plenty of patience and lots of luck!

*Marco von Münchhausen*

# SOME FURTHER READING FOR YOUR LITTLE SABOTEUR

Birkenbihl, Vera F.: *Erfolgstraining. Schaffen Sie sich Ihre Wirklichkeit selbst* [Training for Success: Create Your Own reality]. 12th impression, Landsberg, mvg, 2001

Christiani, Alexander: *Weck den Sieger in Dir! In 7 Schritten zur dauerhaftern Selbstmotivation* [Wake Up the Winner Inside You]. 2nd impression, Wiesbaden, Gabler, 2000

Csikszentmihalyi, Mihaly: *Flow: The Psychology of Optimal Experience.* New York, Harper & Row, 1990

Damasio, Antonio R.: *Descartes' Error: Emotion, Reason and the Human Brain.* New York, Putnam, 1994

DeMarco, Tom: *Slack: Getting Past Burnout, Busywork and the Myth of Total Efficiency.* New York, Random House, 2001

Fiore, Neil: *The Now Habit: A Strategic Program for Overcoming Procrastination and Enjoying Guilt Free Play.* Canberra, Argos Press, 1989

Goleman, Daniel: *Emotional Intelligence.* New York, Bantam Books, 1995

Goulding, Mary McClure: *Who's Been Living in Your Head?* 2nd edition, California, WIGFT Press, 1986

Harms, Meint: *Der innere Schweinehund in Zivil* [The Inner Demon in Civvies], 1954

Johnson, Spencer: *One Minute for Myself: A Small Investment, a Big Reward.* New York, W. Morrow, 1985

Kingston, Karen: *Clear Your Clutter with Feng Shui.* New York, Broadway Books, 1999

Lazarus, Arnold and Fay, Allen: *I Can if I Want To*. Essex, CT, FMC Books, 1999

Löhr, Jörg and Pramann, Ulrich: *Einfach mehr vom Leben. Anleitung für Glück und Erfolg* [Simply More From Life: Instructions for Happiness and Success]. Munich, Südwest, 2000

Rückert, Hans-Werner: *Schluss mit dem ewigen Aufschieben. Wie Sie umsetzen, was Sie sich vornehmen* [Stop Putting It Off: How to Put Your Plans Into Practice]. 3rd impression, Frankfurt/NewYork, Campus, 2000

Seiwert, Lothar J.: *Life-Leadership. Sinnvolles Selbstmanagement für ein Leben in Balance* [Life-Leadership: Sensible Self Management for a Life in Balance]. Frankfurt/NewYork, Campus, 2001

Seiwert, Lothar J.: *Wenn Du es eilig hast, gehe langsam. Das neue Zeitmanagement in einer beschleunigten Welt* [When You Are in a Rush, Go Slowly! Paths Out of Daily Unhappiness]. 7th impression, Frankfurt/NewYork, Campus, 2001

Sprenger, Reinhard K.: *Die Entscheidung liegt bei Dir! Wege aus der täglichen Unzufriedenheit* [The Decision is Yours! How to Deal with Everyday Dissatisfaction]. 9th impression, Frankfurt/NewYork, Campus, 2000

Weinstein, Matt: *Managing to Have Fun*. New York, Simon & Schuster, 1996

Dr. Marco Freiherr von Münchhausen is a lawyer and publisher. He holds seminars and lectures on the topics of motivation, self-management and work–life balance. In researching psychological obstacles on the route to private contentment and top professional performance, he has come across the inner saboteur many times.

# Dr. Marco Freiherr von Münchhausen

is a renowned expert and trainer in the area
of personality and self-management.
He holds presentations and seminars across
Europe on the following themes:

- **Work–life balance**
  How to bring your work and private life into
  harmony.

- **Motivation and stress management**
  How you can reach your goals more effectively
  and with fewer losses to friction.

- **Everyday self-management**
  How you can tame your little saboteurs and even
  befriend them.

- **The activation of your inner resources**
  How you can always recharge your batteries.

Further information and online booking at:
**www.vonmuenchhausen.de**

To receive the full-color book illustrations in poster
or postcard form, as well as further articles on the
subject, please visit

**www.vonmuenchhausen.de**